The Year After...

- 365 days of scripture for the journey of a grieving Heart

Carla Borden

The Year After...

Note from Carla:

My grief journey began one Saturday morning at the age of 32 when I woke up to find my husband laying in the kitchen floor non-responsive. That single moment changed my life forever and if you are experiencing a loss you know that one single moment absolutely can change your life forever. While no one wants to travel this road I can say that through my loss, hurt and pain God has shown me his unconditional love and willingness to walk this road with me.

Through my journey I have discovered some amazing things about God and about myself. One of the many things is I now have an uncommon bond with other women who have suffered the loss of a spouse. I also found that through this experience God is now using me to intercede in prayer for those who grieve. Over the past 20 years I have found that I would have a burden to pray for those who have suffered a loss and that the burden would last a year. Once the year had completed then I felt a release from the daily prayer for them. I never really understood the significance of the year until recently when I learned that in the Jewish faith the children of a widow are asked to meet and pray daily for her the first year. When my daughter shared this with me it truly confirmed to me that this wasn't a coincidence but by divine design.

I believe through this year you too will find how God will take your unspeakable loss and create a beautiful future for you. Remember he gives beauty for ashes.

Prayers, Hugs and Love, Carla

**This book is dedicated to those who started me
on my one year journey.**

My late husband – James Holybee
The day before he passed he said to me, "I don't know what God is
doing but he is getting YOU ready for something big!"

My dear pastor/friends Rick and Rhonda McElhannon
As Rick laid waiting for heaven he taught me that running the race
called Life is not a 40 yard dash but a relay race and at the end you
hand the baton off to the next person to run.

As you journey on this path there will be many people along the way that
God will send to help you. Some people are for a day and some are for a
lifetime, that was true for me as well and two of those people who
became "lifers" were my pastor Rick McElhannon and his wife Rhonda.
Rick preached my husband's funeral, helped me relocate closer to family
and years later officiated at my new marriage. Rhonda took all my late
night phone calls, she cried and laughed with me every step of the way.
Because of my loss, our relationship moved from pastor/friend to
extended family. Twenty years after my husband passed Rick died and my
dear friend Rhonda then too became a widow. I was flooded with so
much emotion because they were so a part of my journey. I so wanted to
be there for her, but now I lived 12 hours away. I knew I had to do
something, so I began to ask God what I could do that would help her the
way she helped me. God said, "Pray for her as you have for all the other
widows." But as if praying wasn't enough I kept pushing God, I wanted to
do something tangible so that she would know I was there for her. I
decided to text or call her every day after I prayed for her, but after a
while I felt like I was invading her space, so I just prayed every day. That
was when the journey of this book began, for Rhonda's first year I
journaled everyday a scripture that God had laid on my heart for her for
the journey. Now her first year has ended and I feel I should share it with
all of those who have a grieving heart.

Things you need to know about reading this book.

1. In my experience at the depths of my grief I couldn't handle a lot of information at one time but I could handle a little daily. So every day there is a little of God's word for you to hold onto as you journey through this year. Of course if you need more just go to that daily scripture in the bible and keep reading.

2. In this dark season I found that looking for one good thing every day that God had provided helped me shift my focus off of me and my loss and onto what I still had. Later I discovered that this practice is actually in 2 Corinthians 10:5," and we take captive every thought to make it obedient to Christ." So I have made a place each day for you to write your one good thing God did for that day.

3. Throughout the 365 days I share a few of my own one good things, thoughts and song suggestions just as a reminder that you are walking a path many have gone on ahead of you, so don't be afraid.

Day 1

Isaiah 54:10

For the mountains may move and the hills disappear, but even then my faithful love for you will remain. My covenant of blessing will never be broken.

Note from Carla: Today's One good thing may be the hardest to find so look for something simple.

On my first day of this journey, I remember the police officer who came back to my house after we left the hospital with his business card in his hand and said, "Please call me if there is anything I can help you with". While the words may seem simple the compassion in his eyes were so strong. I never saw that officer again but that moment has lasted in my heart for over 20 years.

Assignment: Find your ONE good thing for today and write it down. (2 Corinthians 10:5)

_____

_____

Psalm 18:32

It is God who arms me with strength and keeps my way secure.

Note from Carla:

May you find the **strength** to find your ONE good thing for today. The first few days are always noisy, people finding out what has happened, people reaching out to send their condolences or asking how they can help. My Day 2 Good thing was our Youth Pastors who took my daughter's to the bowling alley while I made funeral arrangements.

Assignment: Find your ONE good thing for today and write it down. (2 Corinthians 10:5)

_____

_____

Day 3

Colossians 3:2

Set your minds on things above not on earthly things

Note from Carla:

Although on Day 3 I was still numb and just going through the motions I found my journey revolved around what I could set your mind to just to get through the day. So even though you may feel numb today, set your mind to focus on what God is doing around you.

Assignment: Find your ONE good thing for today and write it down. (2 Corinthians 10:5)

_____

_____

Day 4

Philippians 4:13

I can do ALL things through Christ because he gives me strength –

Note from Carla:
*When I have seen this verse in the past I may have felt it was about winning a race or some great accomplishment but it hit me one day what if **All** means even burying someone I love then know I can do it!*

Assignment: Find your ONE good thing for today and write it down.
(2 Corinthians 10:5)

_____

_____

Day 5

Chronicles 16:11

Look to the Lord and for his strength seek his face always

Note from Carla:
The days seem long right now and I felt so weak but I had to keep my eyes on his face and look for strength in his strength. I basically told him Lord, I can't do this so if we are going to do this you are going to have to make it happen and he did.

Assignment: Find your ONE good thing for today and write it down. (2 Corinthians 10:5)

_____

_____

2 Peter 1:3

His divine power has given us everything we need for a godly life through our knowledge of him who called us by his own glory and goodness

Note from Carla:
God knew this day before it came and he is committed to give us everything we need. For me this day I needed Chicken and Dumplings the best southern comfort food ever made and God provided from a sweet woman named Ms. Robbins.

Assignment: Find your ONE good thing for today and write it down. (2 Corinthians 10:5)

_____

_____

Psalms 9:10

Those who know your name trust in you,
for you, Lord have never forsaken those
who seek you.

Note from Carla:
Woke up this morning with the first thought... it has been
a week! And how I will forever remember the day it
happened and then I blinked and it has been 20 years. But
right now it is just about getting through the day and
remember that the Lord has never forsaken me.

Assignment: Find your ONE good thing for today and write it
down. (2 Corinthians 10:5)

_____

_____

Day 8

Deuteronomy 3:22

Don't be afraid

Note from Carla:
This is a very slow daily walk because everything I knew to be true had now changed. Accepting the change that had occurred tested my faith and I was often afraid.

Assignment: Find your ONE good thing for today and write it down. (2 Corinthians 10:5)

_____

_____

Psalm 27:4

One thing I ask from the Lord, this only do I seek: that I may dwell in the house of the Lord all the days of my life, to gaze on the beauty of the Lord and to seek Him in his temple.

Note from Carla:
These days are dark but there will be a day when there will be no darkness. Praise God!

Assignment: Find your ONE good thing for today and write it down. (2 Corinthians 10:5)

_____

_____

Day 10

Psalms 46:10

Be Still

Note from Carla:
*So many times during this journey I wanted to **run away**!*
I wanted to run from this new life that I had been given
but God kept saying, "Be Still" and know that I am God!

Assignment: Find your ONE good thing for today and write it down. (2 Corinthians 10:5)

_____

_____

Day 11

Isaiah 40:29

He gives power to the weak and strength to
the powerless

Note from Carla:
Prayer today for you to feel God thru your hurt and anger.
Just remember anger is unresolved hurt and you have an
epic size hole in your heart so it's ok...

Assignment: Find your ONE good thing for today and write it
down. (2 Corinthians 10:5)

_____

_____

Day 12

Isaiah 41:10

Don't be afraid, for I am with you, Don't be discouraged for I am your God. I will strengthen you and help you. I will hold you up with my victorious right hand.

Note from Carla:

As I said previously Fear is real on this journey, fear of tomorrow, fear of what to do today, but I love this scripture because God promises to hold you up and help you.

Assignment: Find your ONE good thing for today and write it down. (2 Corinthians 10:5)

_____

_____

Day 13

Psalm 16:8

I keep my eyes always on the Lord. With him at my right hand I will not be shaken.

Note from Carla:
I can remember looking around and thinking I don't understand what is happening or what I am are going to do. But this verse promises that if I keep my eyes on him I will not be shaken.

Assignment: Find your ONE good thing for today and write it down. (2 Corinthians 10:5)

_____

_____

Psalm 34:18

The Lord is close to the brokenhearted and saves those who are crushed in spirit.

Note from Carla:
By now others have gone on with their daily lives while you sit with all your pain, just know God hasn't gone on with his daily life YOU are his daily life.

Assignment: Find your ONE good thing for today and write it down. (2 Corinthians 10:5)

_____

_____

Isaiah 40:28

The Lord is the everlasting God, the Creator of the ends of the earth. He will not grow tired or weary, and his understanding no one can fathom.

Note from Carla:
Though you grow tired and weary God does not! I find such comfort in knowing that he understands me when no one else does.

Assignment: Find your ONE good thing for today and write it down. (2 Corinthians 10:5)

_____

_____

Day 16

Psalm 95:3-5

For the Lord is a mighty God, a mighty king over all god. He rules over the whole earth from the deepest caves to the highest hills. He rules.

Note from Carla:
What a mighty God we serve... What a mighty God we serve! Angels bow before him heaven and Earth adore him what a mighty God we serve. If you don't know this song check it out!

Assignment: Find your ONE good thing for today and write it down. (2 Corinthians 10:5)

_____

_____

Day 17

Mark 5:34B

Go in peace and be freed from your suffering

Note from Carla: Every once and a while I will share a song suggestion. Music soothes my soul in a way nothing else can, I hope it helps you on this journey my music suggestion for today is... Artist: Third Day, Song: "Cry out to Jesus"

Assignment: Find your ONE good thing for today and write it down. (2 Corinthians 10:5)

_____

_____

Day 18

Psalm 37:5-6

Commit your way to the Lord: trust in him
and he will do this: He will make your
righteous reward shine like the dawn, your
vindication like the noonday sun

Note from Carla:
No matter what I have faced I have learned to trust God
because in his time he makes all things right, and he will
vindicate me in the face of those who would do me harm.

Assignment: Find your ONE good thing for today and write it
down. (2 Corinthians 10:5)

_____

_____

Day 19

Psalm 5:12

Surely, Lord, you bless the righteous; you surround them with your favor as with a shield.

Note from Carla

I love this scripture because regardless of how I felt about my circumstances or how overwhelmed I felt the Lord promised to surround me with his favor and be my shield.

Assignment: Find your ONE good thing for today and write it down. (2 Corinthians 10:5)

_____

_____

Day 20

Isaiah 43:19

See I am doing a new thing now it springs up: do you not perceive it? I am making a way in the wilderness and streams in the wasteland

Note from Carla: I can remember feeling like my life was a wilderness and that could easily be forever in this wasteland of sorrow and despair but this verse was God's promise that he was making a way for me.

Assignment: Find your ONE good thing for today and write it down. (2 Corinthians 10:5)

_____

_____

Day 21

Psalm 55:22

Cast your cares on the Lord and he will sustain you; He will never let the righteous be shaken

Note from Carla:
The cares of this journey are daily so I love this scripture because God tells us to cast our cares on him and he will sustain us.

Assignment: Find your ONE good thing for today and write it **down.** (2 Corinthians 10:5)

_____

_____

Psalm 2:8

Ask me, and I will make the nations your inheritance, the ends of the earth your possession.

Note from Carla:
In looking back on what has happened it is hard to comprehend that God has something good ahead. But I am living proof that God wants to give you good things even when all you can see is the bad that has happened.

Assignment: Find your ONE good thing for today and write it down. (2 Corinthians 10:5)

_____

_____

Day 23

Psalm 46:10

Be Still and Know that I am God

Note from Carla:
Being still is something that I am not good at. So when God says
be still that takes real focus for me but by concentrating on the
fact that I know he is God it helps me be still when all I want to
do is move.

Assignment: Find your ONE good thing for today and write it
down. (2 Corinthians 10:5)

_____

_____

Psalm 119:50

Your promise preserves my life

Note from Carla:
My life would be a hot mess without the promises of God. I
hate to think what decisions I would have made without
holding onto the promises of God. Whatever good has become
of my life came from God and his promises.

Assignment: Find your ONE good thing for today and write it
down. (2 Corinthians 10:5)

_____

_____

Day 25

Ephesians 6:10

Be strong in the Lord!

Note from Carla:
Strength comes in many forms what at one time I took for granted like just getting up in the morning now would take strength. Because my brain had now logged that I could wake up and find my husband dead so if that was possible then I could wake up to anything.

Assignment: Find your ONE good thing for today and write it down. (2 Corinthians 10:5)

_____

_____

Day 26

Psalms 73:26

My flesh and my heart may fail, but God is the
strength of my heart and my portion forever

Note from Carla: OK today is a song recommendation,
A great song about this very verse artist Danny Gokey –
"Tell your Heart to beat Again". If you haven't heard it I
strongly recommend it!

Assignment: Find your ONE good thing for today and write it
down. (2 Corinthians 10:5)

_____

_____

Day 27

Psalm 147:3

He heals the Brokenhearted and

Binds up their wounds

Note from Carla:
If ever I needed God to bind up my wounds it was now and I needed him to heal my broken heart because right now my heart was in pieces on the floor.

Assignment: Find your ONE good thing for today and write it down. (2 Corinthians 10:5)

_____

_____

Day 28

1 John 4:18

Fear is Banished.

Note from Carla:
A favorite quote of mine...The Giant in front of you is
never bigger than the God inside of you – Christine Caine
Fear can seem like a giant and God is the giant slayer!

Assignment: Find your ONE good thing for today and write it
down. (2 Corinthians 10:5)

_____

_____

Day 29

Psalm 107:20

He sent out his word and healed them; He rescued them from the grave.

Note from Carla:
I love this because he rescued us from the grave. When the grave is the last place you physically left someone it can be a place that you need to be rescued from. Although preachers will tell you this verse means something else. I believe in our circumstances it applies.

Assignment: Find your ONE good thing for today and write it down. (2 Corinthians 10:5)

_____

_____

Day 30

Psalm 16:6

The boundary lines have fallen for me in pleasant places; surely I have a delightful inheritance.

Note from Carla: The 30 day mark is monumental for this journey. May you spend this day reflecting on the past 30 days and how God has been with you every step.

Assignment: Find your ONE good thing for today and write it down. (2 Corinthians 10:5)

_____

_____

Day 31

Psalm 18:19

He brought me out into a spacious place; he rescued me because he delighted in me.

Note from Carla: I love this promise because he will rescue me and he delights in me, even when I don't. I can remember feeling so closed in by my grief and feeling like I would never see joy again.

Assignment: Find your ONE good thing for today and write it down. (2 Corinthians 10:5)

_____

_____

Psalm 13:5

But I trust in your unfailing love; my heart rejoices in your salvation

Note from Carla:
A quote I found... Sometimes your heart needs more time to accept what your mind already knows.

Assignment: Find your ONE good thing for today and write it down. (2 Corinthians 10:5)

_____

_____

1 John 3:1

See what great love the father has lavished on us, that we should be called children of God

Note from Carla:
May you feel his great love today

Assignment: Find your ONE good thing for today and write it down. (2 Corinthians 10:5)

_____

_____

Day 34

Matthew 5:4

Blessed are those who mourn, for they shall
be comforted

Note from Carla:
What I love about this scripture is that through my
mourning I am blessed not because I mourn but because God
comforts me.

Assignment: Find your ONE good thing for today and write it
down. (2 Corinthians 10:5)

_____

_____

Psalm 34:18

"The Lord is close to the brokenhearted and
saves those crushed in spirit,"

Note from Carla:
By day 35 everyone else in your life may be going about
business as you usual as you are still processing what has
happened. But know that YOU are God's business and he is
close while you are brokenhearted and crushed.

Assignment: Find your ONE good thing for today and write it
down. (2 Corinthians 10:5)

_____

_____

Day 36

Isaiah 66:9

I will not cause pain without allowing
something new to be born says the Lord.

Note from Carla:
I often struggled with how this all worked and what it
meant for me and what good could possibly come from my
life. This verse reminds me that for something new to be
born there is pain. God has born so many things out of my
pain; a ministry, inventions, this book, for God the options
are limitless.

Assignment: Find your ONE good thing for today and write it
down. (2 Corinthians 10:5)

_____

_____

Day 37

Psalm 91:10-11

No Disaster can overtake you, no plague come near your tent; He has given his angels orders about you, to guard you wherever you go.

Note from Carla:
I believe that those who grieve become very aware of the angels that have been ordered about them to guard them wherever they go.

Assignment: Find your ONE good thing for today and write it down. (2 Corinthians 10:5)

_____

_____

Day 38

Psalm 143:8

Let the morning bring me word of your unfailing

love, for I have put my trust in you. Show me the

way I should go, for to you I entrust my life

Note from Carla:

May today you realize once again his unfailing love and
putting your trust in him, the Lord will show you the way
you should go.

Assignment: Find your ONE good thing for today and write it
down. (2 Corinthians 10:5)

_____

_____

Day 39

2 Timothy 4:7

But the Lord stood with me and
gave me strength.

Note from Carla:
When you get overwhelmed by thinking past today
remember All you need is strength for today!

Assignment: Find your ONE good thing for today and write it
down. (2 Corinthians 10:5)

_____

_____

Day 40

Psalm 56:4

In God I trust I shall not be afraid

Note from Carla: I love this song because the lyrics are so honest and really speak to where you may be at Day 40 so please add this to your song list, artists; Lauren Daigle's song "Trust in You"

Assignment: Find your ONE good thing for today and write it down. (2 Corinthians 10:5)

_____

_____

Psalm 56:8

You keep track of all my sorrows, you have
collected all my tears in your bottle.

Note from Carla:
When I think of how many tears I shed over the first 41
days this verse is hard to wrap my mind around.

Assignment: Find your ONE good thing for today and write it
down. (2 Corinthians 10:5)

_____

_____

Day 42

Psalm 9:9-10

The LORD also will be a stronghold for the oppressed, A stronghold in times of trouble; 10.And those who know your name will put their trust in You, For You, O LORD have not forsaken those who seek You.

Assignment: Find your ONE good thing for today and write it down. (2 Corinthians 10:5)

_____

_____

Day 43

Psalm 56:3

We can't always see where the road leads but God promises there's something better up ahead, we have to trust him.

Note from Carla: If ever a scripture describes this journey this scripture does.

Assignment: Find your ONE good thing for today and write it down. (2 Corinthians 10:5)

_____

_____

Day 44

Mark 5:36

Don't be afraid Just believe

Note from Carla: the unknown can bring on the spirit of fear in a way that you may have never experienced before. What is important is to remind yourself that you serve a God who knows everything that is unknown to you, all you have to do is just believe him.

Assignment: Find your ONE good thing for today and write it down. (2 Corinthians 10:5)

_____

_____

2 Kings 20:5

I have heard your prayer and seen your tears
I will heal you

Note from Carla:
Grief is a pain so raw that words cannot describe it and
words cannot console it. Only God can heal a soul so deeply
wounded.

Assignment: Find your ONE good thing for today and write it
down. (2 Corinthians 10:5)

_____

_____

Isaiah 26:3

You will keep in perfect peace all who trust
in you, all those thoughts are fixed on you.

Note from Carla:
Amazing how God can give you peace in a storm when you
trust him. If you don't have peace then pray for it, God
will gladly give it you.

Assignment: Find your ONE good thing for today and write it
down. (2 Corinthians 10:5)

_____

_____

Day 47

Psalm 20:4

May He give you the desire of your heart and
make all your plans succeed

Note from Carla: The thing that was the most difficult for
me was reconciling the desires of my heart. Because the
first real desire of my heart was for none of this to have
happened. So once I got past that what was the desire of my
heart.

Assignment: Find your ONE good thing for today and write it
down. (2 Corinthians 10:5)

_____

_____

Matthew 6:34

So don't worry about tomorrow for tomorrow will bring its own worries. Today's trouble is enough for today.

Note from Carla: This verse has proven true in my life over and over again. I can so get overwhelmed thinking about tomorrow and every time I do God pulls out some miracle the next day and everything I worried about disappears.

Assignment: Find your ONE good thing for today and write it down. (2 Corinthians 10:5)

_____

_____

Day 49

Micah 5:5
He will be our peace

Note from Carla: I hope you find peace in your day.

Assignment: Find your ONE good thing for today and write it down. (2 Corinthians 10:5)

_____

_____

Day 50

Psalm 30:1

I will exalt you, Lord, for you lifted me out of the depths and did not let my enemies gloat over me.

Note from Carla: You may find during this journey that people you thought you could trust are now enemies. Hold on to this verse today and remember for those that walk under God's protection, enemies will not win.

Assignment: Find your ONE good thing for today and write it down. (2 Corinthians 10:5)

_____

_____

Day 51

Psalm 94:19

When the cares of my heart are many, your consolations cheer my soul.

Note from Carla: I hope today your Good thing is laughter. During this journey I found that I laughed about things that others who have not experienced this journey find morbid, but that's ok it is all part of the process. I can laugh about the fact that my child tripped over a coffee table at the funeral home. It was funny!

Assignment: Find your ONE good thing for today and write it down. (2 Corinthians 10:5)

_____

_____

Day 52

1 Corinthians 16:13

Be on your guard; stand firm in the faith be courageous be strong

Note from Carla: Be on your guard to not let the enemy of your soul overtake you, stand firm in your faith, surround yourself with people of faith who will build you up and challenge you in your faith so that you can be courageous and strong.

Assignment: Find your ONE good thing for today and write it down. (2 Corinthians 10:5)

_____

_____

Psalm 22:19

O Lord, Do not stay Far away! You are my strength come quickly to my aid!

Note from Carla: There are days when the Lord seems far away but he is quietly letting you process all that has happened. Know that even in the silence you can call on him for strength and he will come quickly.

Assignment: Find your ONE good thing for today and write it down.
(2 Corinthians 10:5)

_____

_____

Psalm 7:10

My shield is God Most high, who saves the upright in the heart.

Note from Carla: When you feel like you need protecting because maybe you have lost that person who protected you on earth call out this scripture. The most high God is your shield, you are protected.

Assignment: Find your ONE good thing for today and write it down. (2 Corinthians 10:5)

_____

_____

Day 55

John 11: 25

Jesus said to her, "I am the resurrection and the life. The one who believes in me will live, even though they die;

Note from Carla: This journey will cause you to have many encounters that really just can't be explained in the natural. One of my examples was while visiting the National Cemetery where my husband is buried. I went there as much as I could with it being 45 minutes away from where we lived but I kept returning because that was the last place I saw him. One time while standing there it was as if a fog rolled in and I heard a voice as clear as day say," Why are looking for the living among the dead?" then the fog lifted. After that moment I never felt like I had to go to cemetery to be close to him.

Assignment: Find your ONE good thing for today and write it down.
(2 Corinthians 10:5)

_____

_____

Deuteronomy 31:6

Be strong and courageous. Do not be afraid
or terrified because of them, for the Lord
your God goes with you: he will never leave
you nor forsake you.

*Note from Carla: I know you have to be thinking ok Carla
really... how many scriptures are you going to share that
say, "Be Strong, Be courageous, Do not be afraid!" Well
the answer is simple as many as God tells me to share. To
walk this road it is not a one and done sort of deal. You
have to keep saying it.*

Assignment: Find your ONE good thing for today and write it
down. (2 Corinthians 10:5)

_____

_____

Day 57

Lamentations 3:22–23 (NLT)
The faithful love of the Lord never ends! His
mercies never cease. Great is his faithfulness;
his mercies begin afresh each morning.

*Note from Carla: How awesome is it that God's mercies
never cease.*

Assignment: Find your ONE good thing for today and write it
down. (2 Corinthians 10:5)

_____

_____

Day 58

Luke 22:42

Take away the sadness – Saying, Father, if thou be willing, remove this cup from me: nevertheless not my will, but thine, be done.

Note from Carla: Probably one of my greatest requests is for God to take away the sadness, but what if it takes all of this for me to see God and feel him near, then it is worth every minute of it.

Assignment: Find your ONE good thing for today and write it down. (2 Corinthians 10:5)

_____

_____

Day 59

Job 41:22

In his neck remaineth strength, and **sorrow** is turned into joy before him.

Note from Carla: God will turn your sorrow into joy, impossible to believe at this point but just know it is true.

Assignment: Find your ONE good thing for today and write it down. (2 Corinthians 10:5)

_____

_____

Congratulations!

DAY 60!!!

Psalm 3:5

I lie down and sleep; I wake again because the Lord sustains me.

Note from Carla: Every day you wake is because the Lord is sustaining you. Another 30 days have gone by since you started out on this journey. Despite how you feel about it you really are walking this out!

Assignment: Find your ONE good thing for today and write it down. (2 Corinthians 10:5)

_____

_____

Day 61

John 16:24

That your joy may be made full.

Note from Carla: In this journey "JOY" was a tricky thing for me because I would feel somewhat guilty in having joy. As if the loss defined me and I wasn't able to experience true joy again. But God redeemed my sorrow for joy and made it full, you may ask how? Well it wasn't overnight is was over many nights! I remember my.

Assignment: Find your ONE good thing for today and write it down. (2 Corinthians 10:5)

_____

_____

Isaiah 40:31

Those who hope in the Lord will renew their strength. They will soar on wings like eagles; they will run and not grow weary, they will walk and not be faint.

Note from Carla: I love this scripture because of the promises God gives that when I am weak he will renew my strength, that I will soar, that I will run and not get weary and I will walk and not be tired, what incredible promises for this journey.

Assignment: Find your ONE good thing for today and write it down. (2 Corinthians 10:5)

_____

_____

Day 63

John 14:27

I'm leaving you with a gift: peace of mind and heart! And the peace I give isn't fragile like the peace the world gives. So, don't be troubled or afraid.

Note from Carla: Yes, I found another scripture that tells you not to be afraid! But it is important this journey can be scary stuff.

Assignment: Find your ONE good thing for today and write it down. (2 Corinthians 10:5)

_____

_____

Day 64

Revelation 21:4

He will wipe every tear from their eyes. There won't be any more death. There won't be any grief, crying, or pain, because the first things have disappeared.

Note from Carla: Even though 2 months have passed there is still a deep sadness you carry around with you and it is now hard to imagine what it will be like with no grief, crying or pain but MAN will it be awesome!

Assignment: Find your ONE good thing for today and write it down. (2 Corinthians 10:5)

_____

_____

Day 65

Matthew 11:28

Come to me, all who are tired from carrying heavy loads, and I will give you rest.

Note from Carla: I love this because it is exactly what you do while you are grieving you are carrying a heavy load but what a promise that God will give you rest. I remember how hard it was at night. Not being able to sleep without a radio or tv going, so of course I would put on Christian radio or Christian TV because I couldn't handle hearing anything else. I was carrying too much to hear the news, or country songs!

Assignment: Find your ONE good thing for today and write it down. (2 Corinthians 10:5)

_____

_____

Day 66

2 Corinthians 4:16

That is why we are not discouraged. Though outwardly we are wearing out inwardly we are renewed day by day.

Note from Carla: For me the key to this scripture is in the "outwardly we are wearing out" but "inwardly (your spirit man) is renewed day by day" and the more you keep leaning on Jesus for this journey the stronger you will become on the inside.

Assignment: Find your ONE good thing for today and write it down. (2 Corinthians 10:5)

_____

_____

Day 67

Romans 8:18

I consider our present sufferings insignificant compared to the glory that will soon be revealed to us.

Note from Carla: when someone you love has left this earth your present suffering feels anything but insignificant but when you compare it to the glory of the Lord it really brings home how great his glory is if it will make your present suffering insignificant.

Assignment: Find your ONE good thing for today and write it down.
(2 Corinthians 10:5)

_____

_____

Day 68

2 Corinthians 12:9-10

But he told me: "My kindness is all you need. My power is strongest when you are weak." So I will brag even more about my weaknesses in order that Christ's power will live in me. Therefore, I accept weakness, mistreatment, hardship, persecution, and difficulties suffered for Christ. It's clear that when I'm weak, I'm strong.

Assignment: Find your ONE good thing for today and write it down. (2 Corinthians 10:5)

_____

_____

Day 69

Psalm 91:2

He is my God and I trust him

Note from Carla: Even when I don't understand I have to trust him. He is my God and he is trust worthy.

Assignment: Find your ONE good thing for today and write it down. (2 Corinthians 10:5)

_____

_____

Day 70

Psalm 33:13-15

From heaven the Lord looks down and sees all mankind; from his dwelling place he watches all who live on earth- he who forms the hearts of all who considers everything they do.

Note from Carla: Just remember God sees everything and he is watching to see what blessings he can send to you today.

Assignment: Find your ONE good thing for today and write it down. (2 Corinthians 10:5)

_____

_____

Day 71

Psalm 108:13

Through GOD we will do valiantly, For it is
He who shall tread down our enemies

Note from Carla: I love this verse because it says God
will do valiantly. Despite the circumstance my God
will tread down my enemies.

Assignment: Find your ONE good thing for today and write it
down. (2 Corinthians 10:5)

_____

_____

Day 72

Colossians 2: 6

And now, just as you accepted Christ Jesus as your Lord, you must continue to follow him.

Note from Carla: what an incredible scripture for this journey, we must continue to follow him.

Assignment: Find your ONE good thing for today and write it down. (2 Corinthians 10:5)

_____

_____

Day 73

Psalm 143:1

Lord, hear my prayer, listen to my cry for mercy; in your faithfulness and righteousness come to my relief.

Note from Carla: when you look back on your life and what all has happened to you I pray you see God's faithfulness. God knew the day your life would change forever and he had been getting you ready for it even though you had no idea it was coming. That my friend is his faithfulness to you!

Assignment: Find your ONE good thing for today and write it down. (2 Corinthians 10:5)

_____

_____

Day 74

Proverbs 31:25

She is clothed with strength & Dignity she laughs without Fear of the future.

Note from Carla: The day will come when you laugh without fear of the future, without fear of losing someone.

Assignment: Find your ONE good thing for today and write it down. (2 Corinthians 10:5)

_____

_____

Day 75

Psalm 71:20

You have allowed me to suffer much hardship, but you will restore me to life again and lift me up from the depths of the earth.

Note from Carla: To lose someone you love is a suffering that you think can never go away and a hardship you can never recover from but notice in this scripture he says he will lift you up from the depths of the earth.

Assignment: Find your ONE good thing for today and write it down. (2 Corinthians 10:5)

_____

_____

Day 76

Psalm 73:26

My flesh and my heart may fail, but God is the strength of my heart and my portion forever.

Note from Carla: The day of my husband's funeral I stood in my house and said "I can't do this!" I can't bury him. And my family got around me and said "We can do this!" God will give you the strength and so we did. To this day I continue to do things that are impossible with God and his strength.

Assignment: Find your ONE good thing for today and write it **down.** (2 Corinthians 10:5)

_____

_____

Day 77

Romans 15:13

May the God of hope fill you with all joy and peace as you trust in him, so that you may overflow with hope by the power of the Holy Spirit.

Note from Carla: There is this praise song that we would sing," this joy that I have the world didn't give it and the world can't take it away" Notice in this scripture that God will fill you with joy and give you peace so that you may overflow with hope. Having joy is not something you can create it only comes from God.

Assignment: Find your ONE good thing for today and write it down. (2 Corinthians 10:5)

_____

_____

Day 78

John 16:22

So with you: Now is your time of grief, but I will see you again and you will rejoice, and no one will take away your joy.

Note from Carla: Look how at the beginning of this scripture it says "Now is your time of grief" everything has a season.

Assignment: Find your ONE good thing for today and write it down. (2 Corinthians 10:5)

_____

_____

Day 79

Psalm 30:5

For his anger lasts only a moment, but his favor lasts a lifetime; weeping may stay for **the** night, but rejoicing **comes in the morning**.

Note from Carla: What I find interesting about this scripture is that it says weeping may stay (which to me means you don't just get over it!) but rejoicing comes! If you haven't seen any joy yet just hold on it is coming!

Assignment: Find your ONE good thing for today and write it down. (2 Corinthians 10:5)

_____

_____

Day 80

Nehemiah 8:10

This is a sacred day before our Lord. Don't be dejected and sad, for the joy of the LORD is your strength!"

Note from Carla: When I focus on the Lord and begin praying to him about who he is I find joy and strength.

Assignment: Find your ONE good thing for today and write it down. (2 Corinthians 10:5)

_____

_____

Day 81

Colossians 2:7

Let your roots grow down into him, and let your lives be built on him. Then your faith will grow strong in the truth you were taught, and you will overflow with thankfulness.

Note from Carla: Before this journey my roots were superficial but through this my roots have grown deep and my life has been built on him and his goodness towards me. Learning to be thankful for what I have and not what I have lost has been the key.

Assignment: Find your ONE good thing for today and write it down. (2 Corinthians 10:5)

_____

_____

Day 82

John 14:1

"Do not let your hearts be troubled. You believe in God; believe also in me.

Note from Carla: It is difficult to not let your heart be troubled when you have suffered such a loss but God once again says trust me!

Assignment: Find your ONE good thing for today and write it down. (2 Corinthians 10:5)

_____

_____

Day 83

2 Corinthians 1:24

He (God) comforts us whenever we suffer. That is why whenever other people suffer, we are able to comfort them by using the same comfort we have received from God.

Note from Carla: One good thing that has come from what has happened to me is my ability to comfort others who travel this road.

Assignment: Find your ONE good thing for today and write it down. (2 Corinthians 10:5)

_____

_____

Day 84

Matthew 28:20

Lo, I am with you always, even unto the end of the world. Amen.

Note from Carla: Regardless of how I feel I am never alone and neither are you. God is with us always to listen to us, to carry us.

Assignment: Find your ONE good thing for today and write it down. (2 Corinthians 10:5)

_____

_____

Day 85

1 John 4:4

Ye are of God, little children, and have overcome them: because greater is He that is in you, than he that is in the world.

Note from Carla: You are an overcomer! Not because of who you are but because of whose you are!

Assignment: Find your ONE good thing for today and write it down. (2 Corinthians 10:5)

_____

_____

Hebrews 13:5

I will never fail you nor forsake you.

Note from Carla: There were times when I felt that God had failed me and forsaken me. But all the while he was carrying me through this and he understood why I felt the way I did and loved me in spite of it.

Assignment: Find your ONE good thing for today and write it down. (2 Corinthians 10:5)

_____

_____

Day 87

I Peter 5.-10

God, who shows you his kindness and who has called you through Christ Jesus to his eternal glory, will restore you, strengthen you, make you strong, and support you as you suffer for a little while.

Assignment: Find your ONE good thing for today and write it down. (2 Corinthians 10:5)

_____

_____

Day 88

James 5:13

If any of you are having trouble, pray. If you are happy, sing psalms.

Note from Carla: I love this because the answers are simple if you are having trouble PRAY! If you are happy sing!

Assignment: Find your ONE good thing for today and write it down. (2 Corinthians 10:5)

_____

_____

Day 89

Psalms☐ 42☐:11☐

Why am I discouraged? Why is my heart so sad? I will put my hope in God! I will praise him again— my Savior and my God!

Note from Carla: I can remember asking myself these very questions as if my heart would never be happy again. But I had to declare to myself that I would put my hope in God. I would listen to music that built up my faith. I still do it!

Assignment: Find your ONE good thing for today and write it down. (2 Corinthians 10:5)

_____

_____

Day 90

Ephesians 2:8-9

For it is by grace you have been saved through faith. And this is not your own doing; it is the gift of God,

Note from Carla: Just as your salvation was a gift from God, Every day you walk out this journey is a gift to you from God to explore what new thing God is going to do with you. Your journey is just beginning.

Assignment: Find your ONE good thing for today and write it down. (2 Corinthians 10:5)

_____

_____

Day 91

Hebrews 6:15

And so it was that she, having waited long & endured patiently realized and obtained the promise.

Note from Carla: 91 days ago you could have never imagined what God was going to do in your life but know that this is just the beginning for you and that God will do all he has promised.

Assignment: Find your ONE good thing for today and write it down. (2 Corinthians 10:5)

_____

_____

Day 92

Luke 1:45

Blessed is she who has believed that the Lord would fulfill his promises to her.

Note from Carla: There are blessings for believing that the Lord will fulfill his promises regardless how long it takes.

Assignment: Find your ONE good thing for today and write it down. (2 Corinthians 10:5)

_____

_____

Day 93

1 Peter 4:11

If anyone speaks, he should do it as one speaking the very words of God. If anyone serves, he should do it with the strength God provides, so that in all things God may be praised through Jesus Christ. To him be the glory and the power for ever and ever. Amen

Note from Carla: What I love about this scripture is how it addresses what you say and what you do, and your motives. If your actions focus on Christ he will get the glory for it. When God has carried you through the valley you have story to tell, so don't be ashamed to share what God has done.

Assignment: Find your ONE good thing for today and write it down. (2 Corinthians 10:5)

_____

_____

Day 94

Isaiah 55:11

So shall my word be that goeth forth out of my mouth. It shall not return unto me void, but it shall accomplish that which I please and it shall prosper in the thing whereto I sent it.

Note from Carla: The message for me is simple, "Watch your mouth because words are powerful!" Remember that the words spoken by God created the earth.

Assignment: Find your ONE good thing for today and write it down. (2 Corinthians 10:5)

_____

_____

Day 95

Galatians 6:9

Don't get weary in doing good because you will reap in due season.

Note from Carla: During this season I found myself keeping busy so I didn't have time to think about things. While doing good has merit it can make you weary because many things do not have immediate gratification and you are not in season where you have a lot of patience. Listen to what God would have you do so that you know regardless you are doing the good for him and not others.

Assignment: Find your ONE good thing for today and write it down. (2 Corinthians 10:5)

_____

_____

Day 96

Isaiah 41:13

For I am the Lord your God who takes hold of your right hand and says to you, Do not fear; I will help you.

Note from Carla: I love this scripture because I am right handed and love the thought of Jesus literally holding my hand. Amazing how when you are afraid you want to hold someone's hand to be comforted. Here God clearly tells you he is holding your right hand, Do not be afraid.

Assignment: Find your ONE good thing for today and write it down. (2 Corinthians 10:5)

_____

_____

Joshua 1:9

Have I not commanded you? Be strong and courageous. Do not be terrified; do not be discouraged, for the LORD your God will be with you wherever you go.

Note from Carla: After 97 days you may find your life going in directions that terrify and discourage you but know God will be with you wherever you go.

Assignment: Find your ONE good thing for today and write it down. (2 Corinthians 10:5)

_____

_____

Day 98

John 16:33

I have told you these things, so that in me you may have peace. In this world you will have trouble. But take heart! I have overcome the world.

Note from Carla: God is pretty plain, which I appreciate because I have to have it straight. In this world you are going to have trouble! But it's ok because Jesus overcame the world and with him you will too!

Assignment: Find your ONE good thing for today and write it down. (2 Corinthians 10:5)

_____

_____

Day 99

Ephesians 6:11

Put on the full armor of God, so that you can take your stand against the devil's schemes

Note from Carla: After all you have been through you think Satan would just leave you alone but he preys on the weak. that is why it is important to put on the full armor of God so that you can stand! I hope your one good thing today is about how God has helped you stand.

Assignment: Find your ONE good thing for today and write it down. (2 Corinthians 10:5)

_____

_____

Day 100

Romans 12:12

Rejoice in hope, be patient in tribulation, be constant in prayer.

Note from Carla: It was not until I became a widow that I learned how to have a continual on going conversation with God all through the day. But when you are needing his strength to get just get minute by minute the end result is constant prayer.

Assignment: Find your ONE good thing for today and write it down. (2 Corinthians 10:5)

_____

_____

Day 101

Psalm 118:6

The Lord is with me; I will not be afraid

Note from Carla: As you begin your next 100 days know that the Lord is with you every step and while the next 100 days will bring all new challenges and adventures do not be afraid.

Assignment: Find your ONE good thing for today and write it down. (2 Corinthians 10:5)

_____

_____

Day 102

Isaiah 53:4-6

Surely he took up our pain and bore our suffering, yet we considered him punished by God, stricken by him and afflicted. But he was pierced for our transgressions, he was crushed for our iniquities, the punishment that brought us peace was on him and by his wounds we are healed.

Assignment: Find your ONE good thing for today and write it down. (2 Corinthians 10:5)

_____

_____

Day 103

Romans 8:28

And we know that in all things God works for the good of those who love him, who have been called according to his purpose.

Note from Carla: Through this journey I have seen all things work for the good in my life and I am confident that all things will for your good as well.

Assignment: Find your ONE good thing for today and write it **down.** (2 Corinthians 10:5)

_____

_____

Day 104

Luke 21:14

But make up your mind not to worry beforehand how you will defend yourselves.

Note from Carla: I have to make up my mind not to worry and so do you.

Assignment: Find your ONE good thing for today and write it down. (2 Corinthians 10:5)

_____

_____

Day 105

Luke 12:26

Since you cannot do this very little thing, why do you worry about the rest?

Note from Carla:
You can overwhelm yourself with every little thing but God continues to say hand it to him, let him carry it for you.

Assignment: Find your ONE good thing for today and write it **down.** (2 Corinthians 10:5)

_____

_____

Day 106

Ecclesiastes 3:1-2

There is a time for everything, and a season for every activity under heaven.

Note from Carla: What I love about this scripture is that there clearly is a time for everything and while some seasons are short and other seasons are long God has ordained them all.

Assignment: Find your ONE good thing for today and write it down. (2 Corinthians 10:5)

_____

_____

Day 107

Psalm 13:2-4

How long must I wrestle with my thoughts and day after day have sorrow in my heart? Look on my and answer, Lord my God, Give light to my eyes or I will sleep in death, and my enemy will say, "I have overcome him,' and my foes will rejoice when I fall.

Assignment: Find your ONE good thing for today and write it down. (2 Corinthians 10:5)

_____

_____

Day 108

Psalm 119:28

My soul is weary with sorrow; strengthen me according to your word.

Note from Carla:
How well God knows us that he knows your soul is weary with sorrow. I can remember thinking when will I ever feel normal again? And that was when someone told me you will never go back to that normal you will have a new normal. You are forever changed by this event it doesn't define you but it does change you.

Assignment: Find your ONE good thing for today and write it down. (2 Corinthians 10:5)

_____

_____

Day 109

Psalm 116:3-6

The cords of death entangled me, the anguish of the grave came over me; I was overcome by distress and sorrow. Then I called on the name of the Lord: "Lord Save me!" The Lord is gracious and righteous; our God is full of compassion. The Lord protects the unwary; when I was brought low, he saved me.

Assignment: Find your ONE good thing for today and write it down. (2 Corinthians 10:5)

_____

_____

Day 110

Ecclesiastes 1:18

For with much wisdom comes much sorrow;
the more knowledge the more grief.

Note from Carla:
Why share this verse? Because many times during this journey
the truth is hard to face. The truth about your situation, the
truth about what you are facing will make you sad. But know
you can't run from it, knowing the truth brings sorrow but God is
there to comfort you through your sorrow.

Assignment: Find your ONE good thing for today and write it
down. (2 Corinthians 10:5)

_____

_____

Day 111

Isaiah 51:11

Those the Lord has rescued will return. They will enter Zion with singing; everlasting joy will crown their heads. Gladness and joy will overtake them and sorrow and sighing will flee away.

Note from Carla: This verse makes me want to share a song, Artist: Donnie McClurken – Days of Elijah

Assignment: Find your ONE good thing for today and write it down. (2 Corinthians 10:5)

_____

_____

Day 112

Isaiah 60:20

Your sun will never set again, and your moon will wane no more; the Lord will be your everlasting light and your days of sorrow will end.

Assignment: Find your ONE good thing for today and write it down. (2 Corinthians 10:5)

_____

_____

Day 113

Jeremiah 8:18

You who are my Comforter in sorrow, my
heart is faint within me.

*Note from Carla: Pray this verse, remind God of who he is
and remind yourself of who he is.*

Assignment: Find your ONE good thing for today and write it
down. (2 Corinthians 10:5)

_____

_____

The Year After...

Day 114

Jeremiah 31:12-13

They will come and shout for joy on the heights of Zion; they will rejoice in the bounty of the LORD the grain, the new wine and the olive oil, the young of the flocks and herds. They will be like a well-watered garden and they will sorrow no more. Then young women will dance and be glad, young men and old as well. I will turn their mourning into gladness; I will give them comfort and joy instead of sorrow.

Assignment: Find your ONE good thing for today and write it down. (2 Corinthians 10:5)

_____

_____

Day 115

Matthew 14:29-30.

Come, he said. Then Peter got down out of the boat, walked on the water and came toward Jesus. But when he saw the win, he was afraid and beginning to sink, cried out, "Lord, save me!"

Note from Carla: Where you focus your attention makes all the difference. When we get distracted and focus on the circumstances and insurmountable problems in our lives we begin to sink and doubt in our very foundation is challenged, fear of the unknown overwhelmingly starts playing with our minds that Jesus obviously just doesn't care where I am at...Jesus is the author and finisher of our faith..

Assignment: Find your ONE good thing for today and write it down.
(2 Corinthians 10:5)

_____

_____

Day 116

Psalm 102:3-4

For my days vanish like smoke; my bones burn like glowing embers. ⁴ My heart is blighted and withered like grass; I forget to eat my food.

Note from Carla: Playlist suggestion for Day 116, Artist Lauren Daigle song- Come Alive.

Assignment: Find your ONE good thing for today and write it down. (2 Corinthians 10:5)

_____

_____

Day 117

Psalm 102:1

Hear my prayer, LORD;

let my cry for help come to you.

2 Do not hide your face from me

when I am in distress.

Turn your ear to me;

when I call, answer me quickly.

Note from Carla: Playlist suggestion for Day 116 – Artist Whitney Houston song – I Love the Lord. From the album "The Preacher's wife"

Assignment: Find your ONE good thing for today and write it down. (2 Corinthians 10:5)

_____

_____

Day 118

Psalm 120:1

I took my troubles to the Lord;

I cried out to him and he answered my

prayer.

Note from Carla: During this journey you will cry out to God on a daily basis. The Lord wants you to, he wants you to bring your troubles to him, he does not want you to carry them.

Assignment: Find your ONE good thing for today and write it down. (2 Corinthians 10:5)

_____

_____

Day 119

Psalm 100:3

Know that the Lord is God.

It is he who made us, and we are his;

we are his people, the sheep of his pasture.

Assignment: Find your ONE good thing for today and write it down. (2 Corinthians 10:5)

_____

_____

Day 120

Psalm 96 1-3

Sing to the Lord a new song; sing to the Lord, all the earth. Sing to the Lord, praise his name; proclaim his salvation day after day. Declare his glory among the nations, his marvelous deeds among all peoples.

Assignment: Find your ONE good thing for today and write it down. (2 Corinthians 10:5)

_____

_____

Day 121

1 Thessalonians 4:13-14

Brothers and sisters, we do not want you to be uninformed about those who sleep in death, so that you do not grieve like the rest of mankind, who have no hope. For we believe that Jesus died and rose again, and so we believe that God will bring with Jesus those who have fallen asleep.

Assignment: Find your ONE good thing for today and write it down. (2 Corinthians 10:5)

_____

_____

Day 122

Psalm 91:15

He will call on me, and I will answer him; I will be with him in trouble, I will deliver him and honor him.

Note from Carla: What a promise from God that he will answer us and he will be with us in our time of trouble.

Assignment: Find your ONE good thing for today and write it down.
(2 Corinthians 10:5)

_____

_____

Day 123

Psalm 103:6

The Lord works righteousness and justice for all the oppressed.

Note from Carla: there are many times on this journey when it feels like everything is an injustice, no one understands or feels your pain. Just remember this scripture. The Lord is working everything for your good.

Assignment: Find your ONE good thing for today and write it down. (2 Corinthians 10:5)

_____

_____

Day 124

Hebrews 12:1

"Wherefore seeing we also are compassed about with so great a cloud of witnesses, let us lay aside every weight, and the sin which doth so easily beset us, and let us run with patience the race that is set before us"

Note from Carla: Even though your loved one's race has ended yours has not, so run your race.

Assignment: Find your ONE good thing for today and write it down. (2 Corinthians 10:5)

_____

_____

Day 125

Jude 1:2

Everything's going to be all right; rest, everything's coming together; open your hearts, Love is on the way!

Note from Carla: When you read this verse you may think that God has a plan to replace what you lost with exactly what you lost but that is not how God works he is the creator of the universe he is going to do a NEW thing! The Love that is on the way is a New Love! Not a replacement Love.

Assignment: Find your ONE good thing for today and write it down. (2 Corinthians 10:5)

_____

_____

Day 126

Jeremiah 29:11

For I know the thoughts that I think toward you, says the LORD, thoughts of peace and not of evil, to give you a future and a hope. "For promises us 3 things: hope, peace, and a future.

Note from Carla: it's not a coincidence that the enemy does his best to try and destroy your hope with fear

Assignment: Find your ONE good thing for today and write it down. (2 Corinthians 10:5)

_____

_____

Day 127

2 Corinthians 4:7

We are troubled on every side, yet not distressed; we are perplexed but not in despair.

Note from Carla: What I love about this scripture is that it is honest in how it says you have TROUBLE but it doesn't have you!

Assignment: Find your ONE good thing for today and write it down. (2 Corinthians 10:5)

_____

_____

Deuteronomy 31:8

The LORD himself goes before you and will be
with you; he will never leave you nor forsake
you. Do not be afraid; do not be discouraged.

*Note from Carla: The Lord goes ahead of us and will be
with us; HE alone will never leave us.*

Assignment: Find your ONE good thing for today and write it
down. (2 Corinthians 10:5)

_____

_____

Day 129

Psalm 119:76
May your unfailing love be my comfort,
according to your promise to your servant.

Note from Carla: God's love is unfailing for us.

Assignment: Find your ONE good thing for today and write it
down. (2 Corinthians 10:5)

_____

_____

Psalm 138:8

The Lord will vindicate me; your love, Lord,
endures forever- do not abandon the works
of your hands.

*Note from Carla: Just try to soak up and feel the Love
that endures forever.*

Assignment: Find your ONE good thing for today and write it
down. (2 Corinthians 10:5)

_____

_____

Day 131

Psalm 27:1

The Lord is my light and my salvation; whom shall I fear? The LORD is the strength of my life; of whom shall I be afraid?

Note from Carla: Never forget the Lord is your strength.

Assignment: Find your ONE good thing for today and write it down. (2 Corinthians 10:5)

_____

_____

Day 132

Psalm 37:39

But the salvation of the righteous is from the
Lord: He is their strength in time of trouble.

*Note from Carla: The Lord is your strength for this
journey so when you don't feel you can take another
step just let God carry you.*

Assignment: Find your ONE good thing for today and write it
down. (2 Corinthians 10:5)

_____

_____

Day 133

Matthew 19:26

But Jesus looked at them and said to them, with men this is impossible, but with God all things are impossible.

Note from Carla: I can't even tell you how many days I have looked at my situation and thought on my own it was impossible but then God did the impossible!

Assignment: Find your ONE good thing for today and write it down. (2 Corinthians 10:5)

_____

_____

Day 134

2 Timothy 1:7

For God has not given us a spirit of fear, but
of power and of love and of a sound mind.

Note from Carla: Let this scripture be your prayer today.
Memorize it and repeat it to yourself. Many things on this
journey will challenge your spirit and make your feel powerless
and make you feel like you are losing your mind but 2 Timothy
is your anchor to hold to!

Assignment: Find your ONE good thing for today and write it
down. (2 Corinthians 10:5)

_____

_____

Day 135

Isaiah 9:7

"Of the increase of His government and peace there will be no end, upon the throne of David and over His kingdom, to order it and establish it with judgment and justice from that time forward, even forever more. The zeal of the Lord of hosts will perform this."

Note from Carla: To know that there will be a day where Peace will have no end brings comfort to me and I hope you as well.

Assignment: Find your ONE good thing for today and write it down. (2 Corinthians 10:5)

_____

_____

Day 136

Isaiah 11:9

They shall not hurt or destroy in all my holy mountain for the earth shall be full of the knowledge of the LORD as the waters cover the sea.

Note from Carla: I have seen hurt and have seen things destroyed that I couldn't wrap my mind around and then when I was ready the Lord revealed to me knowledge that helped me understand my hurt.

Assignment: Find your ONE good thing for today and write it down. (2 Corinthians 10:5)

_____

_____

Day 137

Daniel 12:3

Those who are wise shall shine like the brightness of the firmament and those who turn many to righteousness like the stars forever and ever.

Note from Carla: How cool to know that this life has impact even after your life has stopped on this earth.

Assignment: Find your ONE good thing for today and write it down. (2 Corinthians 10:5)

_____

_____

Day 138

Micah 4:4

But everyone shall sit under his vine and under his fig tree, and no one shall make them afraid; for the mouth of the mouth of the LORD of hosts has spoken.

Note from Carla: Be encouraged God will provide and he will protect.

Assignment: Find your ONE good thing for today and write it down. (2 Corinthians 10:5)

_____

_____

Day 139

Zephaniah 3:17

The LORD your God in your midst, the
Mighty One, will save; He will rejoice over
you with gladness, He will quite you with his
love, he will rejoice over you with singing.

*Note from Carla: It just makes my heart sing to read
that the Lord is in my midst. Even if you are angry
with him because of your circumstances he is in your
midst and he loves you.*

Assignment: Find your ONE good thing for today and write it
down. (2 Corinthians 10:5)

_____

_____

Day 140

1 Corinthians 2:9

"Eye has not seen, nor ear heard, nor have entered into the heart of man the things which God has prepared for those who love Him."

Note from Carla: What God has planned for you is beyond anything you can dream or imagine, so hold on and keep loving God.

Assignment: Find your ONE good thing for today and write it down. (2 Corinthians 10:5)

_____

_____

Day 141

Peter 1:10-11

"Therefore, brethren, be even more diligent to make your call and election sure, for if you do these things you will never stumble; for so an entrance will be supplied to you abundantly into the everlasting kingdom of our Lord and Savior Jesus Christ."

Note from Carla: On this journey every step is scary and every step makes your question your ability but be diligent in your request to God and you will not stumble.

Assignment: Find your ONE good thing for today and write it down. (2 Corinthians 10:5)

_____

_____

Day 142

1 John 3:2

"Beloved, now we are children of God; and it has not yet been revealed what we shall be, but we know that when He is revealed, we shall be like Him, for we shall see Him as He is."

Note from Carla: Right now you really don't know what shall be but know he will reveal it.

Assignment: Find your ONE good thing for today and write it down. (2 Corinthians 10:5)

_____

_____

Day 143

Revelation 21:13

I am the Alpha and the Omega, the First
And the Last, the Beginning and the End.

Note from Carla: sometimes you just need to be
reminded that God is the beginning and the end,
So as you are in the middle he is with you and he
knows everything.

Assignment: Find your ONE good thing for today and write it
down. (2 Corinthians 10:5)

_____

_____

Day 144

Psalm 23:4, 6

"Yea, though I walk through the valley of the shadow of death, I will fear no evil; for You are with me; Your rod and Your staff, they comfort me. … Surely goodness and mercy shall follow me all the days of my life; and I will dwell in the house of the LORD forever."

Note from Carla: Until James died I never truly understood the valley of the shadow of death, but this verse means more to me now that it ever has.

Assignment: Find your ONE good thing for today and write it down. (2 Corinthians 10:5)

_____

_____

Day 145

Isaiah 40:1

"Comfort, yes, comfort My people!' says your God."

Note from Carla: God wants to comfort you, he feels your loss and knows that you hurt.

Assignment: Find your ONE good thing for today and write it down. (2 Corinthians 10:5)

_____

_____

Day 146

Romans 15:4

"For whatever things were written before were written for our learning, that we through the patience and comfort of the Scriptures might have hope."

Note from Carla: I love this verse because God's word gives me hope in every situation.

Assignment: Find your ONE good thing for today and write it down. (2 Corinthians 10:5)

_____

_____

Day 147

2 Corinthians 1:3

"Blessed be the God and Father of our Lord Jesus Christ, the Father of mercies and God of all comfort."

Note from Carla: I am so glad Jesus Christ is the father of mercies and God of all comfort. Because the pain is as real at day 147 as it was at day 1.

Assignment: Find your ONE good thing for today and write it down. (2 Corinthians 10:5)

_____

_____

Day 148

Psalm 103:13-14

"As a father pities his children, so the LORD pities those who fear Him. For He knows our frame; He remembers that we are dust."

Note from Carla: I love that the Lord understands how fragile I am and that I am just dirt.

Assignment: Find your ONE good thing for today and write it down. (2 Corinthians 10:5)

_____

_____

Day 149

Romans 8:35

"Who shall separate us from the love of Christ? Shall tribulation, or distress, or persecution, or famine, or nakedness, or peril, or sword?"

Note from Carla: In this moment you can feel so separated from everyone and everything but NOTHING can separate you from the love of Christ.

Assignment: Find your ONE good thing for today and write it down. (2 Corinthians 10:5)

_____

_____

Day 150

Romans 8:37-39

"Yet in all these things we are more than conquerors through Him who loved us. For I am persuaded that neither death nor life, nor angels nor principalities nor powers, nor things present nor things to come, nor height nor depth, nor any other created thing, shall be able to separate us from the love of God which is in Christ Jesus our Lord."

Assignment: Find your ONE good thing for today and write it down. (2 Corinthians 10:5)

_____

_____

Day 151

Peter 5:6-7

"Therefore humble yourselves under the mighty hand of God, that He may exalt you in due time, casting all your care upon Him, for He cares for you."

Note from Carla: Today is your daily reminder to cast all of your cares on Jesus!

Assignment: Find your ONE good thing for today and write it down. (2 Corinthians 10:5)

_____

_____

Day 152

Nahum 1:7

The Lord is good, a stronghold in the day of trouble; and he knows those who trust in him.

Note from Carla: God knows if you trust him, he will be your stronghold. Many times you have to just tell God that you trust him not for him but for you!

Assignment: Find your ONE good thing for today and write it down. (2 Corinthians 10:5)

_____

_____

Day 153

Exodus 14:13-14

"And Moses said to the people, 'Do not be afraid. Stand still, and see the salvation of the LORD, which He will accomplish for you today. For the Egyptians whom you see today, you shall see again no more forever. The LORD will fight for you, and you shall hold your peace.'"

Note from Carla: Today is your reminder is that God will fight for you!

Assignment: Find your ONE good thing for today and write it down. (2 Corinthians 10:5)

_____

_____

Day 154

Psalm 34:19

"Many are the afflictions of the righteous, but the LORD delivers him out of them all."

Note from Carla: What I love about this scripture is that it says many are the afflictions, because many things have happened to me but the Lord promises to deliver me from them all!

Assignment: Find your ONE good thing for today and write it down. (2 Corinthians 10:5)

_____

_____

Day 155

Psalm 91:7

"A thousand may fall at your side, and ten thousand at your right hand; but it shall not come near you."

Note from Carla: This scripture speaks to God's protection over you, through this loss you may feel like you have lost your protection or your person who provided that but God steps in and says I will be your protection!

Assignment: Find your ONE good thing for today and write it down. (2 Corinthians 10:5)

_____

_____

Day 156

2 Corinthians 4:8-9

"We are hard-pressed on every side, yet not crushed; we are perplexed, but not in despair; persecuted, but not forsaken; struck down, but not destroyed."

Words from my friend Rick who passed in 2016:

Just a reminder you can be in what seems like the worse circumstances you have ever been in and feel like things are totally hopeless--- yet when you have placed your trust in the Lord, it is amazing what he can bring you through—He can do more in one day for you than what the enemy has tried to do your entire life.

Assignment: Find your ONE good thing for today and write it down. (2 Corinthians 10:5)

_____

_____

Day 157

Proverbs 16:7

"When a man's ways please the LORD, He makes even his enemies to be at peace with him."

Note from Carla: We all have enemies for various reason but when we respond like Jesus to them they have no recourse but to be at peace with us.

Assignment: Find your ONE good thing for today and write it down. (2 Corinthians 10:5)

_____

_____

Day 158

Philippians 4:6-7

"Be anxious for nothing, but in everything by prayer and supplication, with thanksgiving, let your requests be made known to God; and the peace of God, which surpasses all understanding, will guard your hearts and minds through Christ Jesus."

Note from Carla: I have been anxious for everything but prayed and thanked God and submitted by request and in doing so my anxiousness would disappear.

Assignment: Find your ONE good thing for today and write it down. (2 Corinthians 10:5)

_____

_____

Day 159

Psalm 46:1

"God is our refuge and strength, a very present help in trouble."

Note from Carla: This is your daily reminder that God is your refuge and your strength.

Assignment: Find your ONE good thing for today and write it down. (2 Corinthians 10:5)

_____

_____

Day 160

Proverbs 3:5

"Trust in the LORD with all your heart, and lean not on your own understanding.

Note from Carla: I cannot stress enough how trusting God is a daily decision. Do not try to understand what has happened, just trust God to help you walk this out.

Assignment: Find your ONE good thing for today and write it down. (2 Corinthians 10:5)

_____

_____

Day 161

Hebrews 4:15-16

"For we do not have a High Priest who cannot sympathize with our weaknesses, but was in all points tempted as we are, yet without sin. Let us therefore come boldly to the throne of grace, that we may obtain mercy and find grace to help in time of need."

Note from Carla: I love that God says come boldly to the throne of grace because he understands your need and wants you to come to him for help.

Assignment: Find your ONE good thing for today and write it down. (2 Corinthians 10:5)

_____

_____

Day 162

Hebrews 13:6

So we say with confidence, "The Lord is my helper; I will not fear. What can man do to me?"

Note from Carla: When God's got your back you, you got this!

Assignment: Find your ONE good thing for today and write it down. (2 Corinthians 10:5)

_____

_____

Day 163

Psalm 61:8

Trust in Him at all times, Pour out your heart before him, God is a refuge for us.

Note from Carla: One of the benefits for me on this journey was I learned how to pour out my heart daily to God. I was so wounded by the loss that He was my only refuge. Friends and family were there for me but only God really got the level of my pain.

Assignment: Find your ONE good thing for today and write it down. (2 Corinthians 10:5)

_____

_____

Day 164

2 Corinthians 4:1

The best of men would faint, if they did not receive mercy from God. And that mercy which has helped us out, and helped us on, hitherto, we may rely upon to help us even to the end.

Note from Carla: I believe there are some stresses that you literally can't physically hold up under but God will help you even to the end!

Assignment: Find your ONE good thing for today and write it down. (2 Corinthians 10:5)

_____

_____

Day 165

Ephesians 4:2

Be completely humble and gentle; be patient bearing with one another in love.

Note from Carla: When your burden feels so heavy you can often find it impossible to bear other people or their burdens, so my recommendation is pray this scripture that God will help you be patient bearing with one another in love.

Assignment: Find your ONE good thing for today and write it down. (2 Corinthians 10:5)

_____

_____

Day 166

John 15:13

Greater love has no one than this: to lay down one's life for one's friends.

Note from Carla: You know from some this scripture is literal they have died for another but this can also mean that you show no greater love than when you lay down your wants for another.

Assignment: Find your ONE good thing for today and write it down. (2 Corinthians 10:5)

_____

_____

Day 167

Deuteronomy 10:17-18

For the LORD your God is God of gods and Lord of lords, the great God, mighty and awesome, who shows no partiality and accepts no bribes. He defends the cause of the fatherless and the widow, and loves the foreigner residing among you, giving them food and clothing.

Assignment: Find your ONE good thing for today and write it down. (2 Corinthians 10:5)

_____

_____

Day 168

Deuteronomy 11: 13-15

So if you faithfully obey the commands I am giving you today- to love the LORD your God and to serve him with all your heart and with all your soul- 14 then I will send rain on your land in its season, both autumn and spring rains, so that you may gather in your grain, new wine and olive oil. I will provide grass in the fields for your cattle and you will eat and be satisfied.

Assignment: Find your ONE good thing for today and write it down. (2 Corinthians 10:5)

_____

_____

Day 169

Hebrews 6:19

Hope anchors the soul

Note from Carla: Hope is only something that God can give you and will anchor your soul.

Assignment: Find your ONE good thing for today and write it down. (2 Corinthians 10:5)

_____

_____

Day 170

Hosea 2:15

God is the only one who can make the valley of trouble a door of hope.

Note from Carla: This verse speaks truth to your journey, only God can make this valley you are walking through a door of hope for you.

Assignment: Find your ONE good thing for today and write it down. (2 Corinthians 10:5)

_____

_____

Day 171

Hebrews 10:23

Let us hold fast the confession of our Hope without wavering for he who promised is faithful abounding Hope.

Note from Carla: Hold onto God's promise even when everything around you feels hopeless!

Assignment: Find your ONE good thing for today and write it down. (2 Corinthians 10:5)

_____

_____

Day 172

Psalm 39:7

But now, Lord what do I look for?

My hope is in you.

Note from Carla; Song for your Playlist, Artist- Big Daddy Weave, Song-Redeemed.

Assignment: Find your ONE good thing for today and write it down. (2 Corinthians 10:5)

_____

_____

Day 173

Psalm 4:8

I will both lay me down in peace, and sleep: for thou, LORD, only makest me dwell in safety.

Note from Carla: On this journey laying down in peace and sleeping can be a challenge but the Lord will keep you in peace and give you rest. Just ask for his help!

Assignment: Find your ONE good thing for today and write it down. (2 Corinthians 10:5)

_____

_____

Day 174

Romans 8:24

But hope that is seen is no hope at all. Who hopes for what they already have?

Note from Carla: Hope is an interesting thing, the things you hoped for before you started this journey were probably very different than what you hope for now. I know that was true for me.

Assignment: Find your ONE good thing for today and write it down. (2 Corinthians 10:5)

_____

_____

Day 175

Psalm 138:3

In the day when I cried out. You answered me and made me bold with strength in my soul.

Note from Carla: In these past 175 days you have had strength that you never imagined possible because you cried out to God and he answered you.

Assignment: Find your ONE good thing for today and write it down. (2 Corinthians 10:5)

_____

_____

Day 176

2 Samuel 22:33

God is my strength and power: and he maketh my way perfect.

Note from Carla: God is perfecting your path.

Assignment: Find your ONE good thing for today and write it down. (2 Corinthians 10:5)

_____

_____

Day 177

Habakkuk 3:19

The LORD God is my strength, and he will make my feet like hinds' feet, and he will make me to walk upon mine high places.

Note from Carla: When I was walking in the valley of the shadow of death I could not imagine walking in high places.

Assignment: Find your ONE good thing for today and write it down. (2 Corinthians 10:5)

_____

_____

Day 178

Isaiah 43:4

Because you are precious in my eyes, and honored and I love you.

Note from Carla: For as much as you love the one you lost God loves you more!

Assignment: Find your ONE good thing for today and write it down. (2 Corinthians 10:5)

_____

_____

Day 179

Psalm 28:7-8

The LORD is my strength and my shield; my heart trusts in him, and he helps me. My heart leaps for joy and with my song I praise him. The LORD is the strength of his people a fortress of salvation for his anointed one.

Assignment: Find your ONE good thing for today and write it down. (2 Corinthians 10:5)

_____

_____

Psalm 54:4

Surely God is my help the Lord is the one who sustains me.

Note from Carla: Many people will try to help you on this journey but only the help of the Lord will sustain you!

Assignment: Find your ONE good thing for today and write it down. (2 Corinthians 10:5)

_____

_____

Day 181

Isaiah 43:2

When you pass through the waters, I will be with you; and when you pass through the rivers, they will not sweep over you. When you walk through the fire, you will not be burned the flames will not set you ablaze.

Note from Carla: Song for your Playlist, Artist-Crowder, Song- Come As You Are.

Assignment: Find your ONE good thing for today and write it down. (2 Corinthians 10:5)

_____

_____

Day 182

Psalm 30:11

You have turned my mourning into joyful dancing. You have taken away my clothes of mourning and clothed me with joy, that I might sing praises to you and not be silent. O LORD my God, I will give you thanks forever!"

Note from Carla: It is hard to imagine at the 6 month point that God could possibly turn your mourning into joyful dancing but when it's time he will take away your clothes of mourning and cloth you with joy that you will sing his praises and you will not be able to be silent about the works of the Lord!

Assignment: Find your ONE good thing for today and write it down. (2 Corinthians 10:5)

_____

_____

Day 183

Isaiah 43:5

Fear not, for I am with you.

Note from Carla: Knowing that you are not alone on this journey is something that will sustain you and when fear comes you will go directly to the peacemaker.

Assignment: Find your ONE good thing for today and write it down. (2 Corinthians 10:5)

_____

_____

Day 184

Psalm 118:14

The LORD is my strength and my defense he has become my salvation.

Note from Carla: This scripture will be your testimony that through this journey the Lord is your strength.

Assignment: Find your ONE good thing for today and write it down. (2 Corinthians 10:5)

_____

_____

Day 185

Isaiah 12:2

Surely God is my salvation; I will trust and not be afraid. The LORD the LORD himself, is my strength and my defense; he has become my salvation.

Note from Carla: This day will hold many challenges but I will trust and not be afraid.

Assignment: Find your ONE good thing for today and write it down.
(2 Corinthians 10:5)

_____

_____

Day 186

Isaiah 33:2

LORD, be gracious to us; we long for you. Be our strength every morning, our salvation in time of distress.

Assignment: Find your ONE good thing for today and write it down. (2 Corinthians 10:5)

_____

_____

Day 187

Isaiah 41:14

Do not be afraid, do not fear, for I myself will help you, declares the Lord.

Note from Carla: The bible is full of scripture about being afraid for a reason! Because fear is something that we all deal with and God is constantly telling us that he is with you! You are not alone!

Assignment: Find your ONE good thing for today and write it down.
(2 Corinthians 10:5)

_____

_____

Day 188

Ephesians 3:16

I pray that out of his glorious riches he may strengthen you with power through his Spirit in your inner being.

Note from Carla: This is my prayer for you today!

Assignment: Find your ONE good thing for today and write it down. (2 Corinthians 10:5)

_____

_____

Day 189

Isaiah 6:3

And one called to another and said:
"Holy, holy, holy is the Lord of hosts; the whole
earth is full of his glory!"

*Note from Carla; Song for your Playlist, Artist-Casting
Crowns, Song-Glorious Day*

Assignment: Find your ONE good thing for today and write it down.
(2 Corinthians 10:5)

_____

_____

Day 190

Psalm 31:24

Be strong and take heart, all you who hope in the LORD.

Note from Carla: While on this journey I have had trust issues and felt weak and felt like I could never hope again but the Lord carried me when I couldn't be strong and he is my only hope.

Assignment: Find your ONE good thing for today and write it down. (2 Corinthians 10:5)

_____

_____

Day 191

Psalm 121:1-2

I will lift mine eyes into the hills, from whence cometh my help. My help cometh from the Lord, which made heaven and earth.

Note from Carla: A Song for your music Playlist today.

Tauren Wells, "Hills & Valleys"

Assignment: Find your ONE good thing for today and write it down.
(2 Corinthians 10:5)

_____

_____

Day 192

Psalm 37:4

Take delight in the LORD, and he will give
you the desires of your heart.

*Note from Carla: It was Hard for me to imagine that
he would give me the desires of my heart when on that
Saturday morning my plan was to go out for
Breakfast with my family not choose a funeral
home. The point of this verse for me was to focus on the
Lord and find his goodness and he would show me the
desires of my heart.*

Assignment: Find your ONE good thing for today and write it
down. (2 Corinthians 10:5)

_____

_____

Day 193

Psalm 18:2

The Lord is my rock, and my safe place, and the One Who takes me out of trouble. My God is my rock, in whom I am safe. He is my safe-covering, my saving strength, and my strong tower

Note from Carla: It is my prayer that this scripture will be your testimony when you talk about this year journey. That you will be able to say with unwavering confidence the Lord is my Rock!

Assignment: Find your ONE good thing for today and write it down.
(2 Corinthians 10:5)

_____

_____

Day 194

Matthew 7:7

"Ask and it will be given to you; seek, and you will find; knock and it will be opened to you."

Note from Carla: During this year journey doors have opened that only God could make possible. You have 194 days of good things and I am sure doors that have opened for you have been many of them.

Assignment: Find your ONE good thing for today and write it down. (2 Corinthians 10:5)

_____

_____

Day 195

Proverbs 22:4 (NLT)
True humility and fear of the Lord lead to riches,
honor, and long life.

*Note from Carla: Why share this scripture? Because I
believe one of the greatest gifts of this journey is true
humility and understanding you are not in control and the
Lord is and understanding that will bring good things to you.*

Assignment: Find your ONE good thing for today and write it down.
(2 Corinthians 10:5)

_____

_____

Day 196

Proverbs 4:25

Let your eyes look directly forward, and your gaze be straight before you.

Note from Carla: On this journey you will always want to go back to the way things were before it all happened instead of looking forward. But take this scripture as your guide keep your eyes forward!

Assignment: Find your ONE good thing for today and write it down. (2 Corinthians 10:5)

_____

_____

Day 197

Psalm 34:8

Taste and See that the Lord is Good.

Note from Carla: While many things on this journey have been so painful the goodness of the Lord has shown through it all, whether from a kind word from a friend or just a beautiful sunrise, God is good!

Assignment: Find your ONE good thing for today and write it down.
(2 Corinthians 10:5)

_____

_____

Psalm 46:5

God is within her, she will not fall.

Note from Carla: On this journey never letting go of the hand of God is key!

Assignment: Find your ONE good thing for today and write it down. (2 Corinthians 10:5)

_____

_____

Day 199

Psalm 61:2-4

From the end of the earth I call to You when my heart is faint; Lead me to the rock that is higher than I. 3 For You have been a refuge for me, A tower of strength against the enemy. 4. Let me dwell in your tent forever; Let me take refuge in the shelter of Your wings. Selah....

Assignment: Find your ONE good thing for today and write it down.
(2 Corinthians 10:5)

_____

_____

Day 200

Psalm 59:9

Because of his strength I will watch for You,
For God is my stronghold.

Note from Carla: For 200 days you have proven the strength of God by doing the simple things through your pain and loss.

Assignment: Find your ONE good thing for today and write it down. (2 Corinthians 10:5)

_____

_____

Day 201

Proverbs 18:10

The name of the Lord is a strong tower; The righteous runs into it and is safe.

Note from Carla: Man is this verse ever true of this journey. The Lord is a strong tower and you running to him for safety is how you have sustained.

Assignment: Find your ONE good thing for today and write it down.
(2 Corinthians 10:5)

_____

_____

Day 202

Psalm 62:7

On God my salvation and my glory rest; The rock of my strength my refuge is in God.

Note from Carla: I have heard it said many times, "How will we make it without them they were the rock of our family?" and losing that person can be devastating but the Lord wants to be your rock because he is everlasting.

Assignment: Find your ONE good thing for today and write it down. (2 Corinthians 10:5)

_____

_____

Day 203

Psalm 71:7

I have become a marvel to many,

For YOU are my strong refuge.

Note from Carla: I so identify with this verse because I knew no one that was a widow at 32, so many of the widows that I met were in their 70's and would just marvel at me. In that moment they would have great sadness for me because of the years they had with their husband that I didn't get but then you could just see the gratitude they felt in that moment for all the years they did get with their spouse. It was a very strange but cool thing to watch.

Assignment: Find your ONE good thing for today and write it down.
(2 Corinthians 10:5)

_____

_____

Day 204

Isaiah 46:3-4

3. "Listen to Me, O house of Jacob, and all the remnant of the house of Israel, You who have been borne by me from birth and have been carried from the womb; 4. Even to your old age I will be the same, And even to your graying years I will bear you! I have done it, and I will carry you; And I will bear you and I will deliver you...

Assignment: Find your ONE good thing for today and write it down. (2 Corinthians 10:5)

_____

_____

Day 205

Deuteronomy 1:30-31

30. 'The LORD your God who goes before you will Himself fight on your behalf, just as He did for you in Egypt before your eyes, 31. And in the wilderness where you saw how the LORD your God carried you, just as a man carries his son, in all the way which you have walked until you came to this place.

Assignment: Find your ONE good thing for today and write it down. (2 Corinthians 10:5)

_____

_____

Day 206

Isaiah 60:1

Arise, shine: For your light has come!
And the glory of the Lord is risen upon
you.

*Note from Carla: In the darkness it is hard to
see the light but the glory of the Lord will rise
upon you!*

Assignment: Find your ONE good thing for today and
write it down. (2 Corinthians 10:5)

_____

_____

Day 207

Psalm 32:7

You are my hiding place; You preserve me from trouble; You surround me with songs of deliverance. Selah

Note from Carla; Song for your music Playlist today, Artist-Kristine DeMarco, Song-I am No Victim.

Assignment: Find your ONE good thing for today and write it down. (2 Corinthians 10:5)

_____

_____

Psalm 130:7

Hope in the Lord: for with the Lord there is
unfailing Love, his redemption overflows.

Assignment: Find your ONE good thing for today and write it
down. (2 Corinthians 10:5)

_____

_____

Day 209

Matthew 21:22

If you *believe* you will *receive* whatever you ask for in *prayer.*

Note from Carla: Some people look at this like a Jeanie in a bottle but I believe there are 3 key words in this verse; believe, receive, pray.

Assignment: Find your ONE good thing for today and write it down. (2 Corinthians 10:5)

_____

_____

Day 210

Esther 4:14

Perhaps this is the moment for which you have been created.

Note from Carla: What if this moment was exactly what you were created for?

Assignment: Find your ONE good thing for today and write it down. (2 Corinthians 10:5)

_____

_____

Day 211

Zechariah 2:5

And I will be to her a wall of Fire all around declares the lord and I will be the glory in her midst.

Note from Carla: What an incredible image that God would be a wall of fire all around you protecting you!

Assignment: Find your ONE good thing for today and write it down. (2 Corinthians 10:5)

_____

_____

Day 212

Romans 5:8

You are loved more than you will ever know by someone who died to know you.

Note from Carla: I pray today you feel how much you are loved by the one who died for you.

Assignment: Find your ONE good thing for today and write it down. (2 Corinthians 10:5)

_____

_____

Day 213

Psalm 62:5-6

Yes, my soul, find rest in God; my hope comes from him. Truly he is my rock and my salvation; he is my fortress, I will not be shaken.

Note from Carla: May your soul find rest today.

Assignment: Find your ONE good thing for today and write it down. (2 Corinthians 10:5)

_____

_____

Day 214

Hebrews 6:10

God is not unjust; he will not forget your work and the love you have shown him as you have helped his people and continue to help them.

Note from Carla: People forget what you have done but God never forgets!

Assignment: Find your ONE good thing for today and write it down. (2 Corinthians 10:5)

_____

_____

Day 215

Joshua 3:4

Then you will know which way to go, since
You have never gone this way before.

*Note from Carla: Music for your Playlist today
Jeremy Camp, "Walk by Faith"-
He too has been on this road.*

Assignment: Find your ONE good thing for today and write it
down. (2 Corinthians 10:5)

_____

_____

Day 216

Joshua 3:5

Consecrate yourselves for tomorrow the Lord
will do amazing things among you.

Note from Carla: I stand amazed at what God has
done for me since the loss of my husband, losing him
was not the only valley I would see in my life but God
continues to do amazing things to prove that the
valley is just a passing through place not a
destination.

Assignment: Find your ONE good thing for today and write it
down. (2 Corinthians 10:5)

_____

_____

Day 217

Hebrews 11:1

Now Faith is confidence in what we
hope for and assurance about what we do
not see.

*Note from Carla; Song for your Playlist today,
Artist- Switchfoot, Song-I won't let you go.*

Assignment: Find your ONE good thing for today and write it
down. (2 Corinthians 10:5)

_____

_____

Day 218

Ecclesiastes 2:26

To the person who pleases him, God gives wisdom, knowledge and happiness, but to the sinner he gives the task of gathering and storing up wealth to hand it over to the one who pleases God.

Note from Carla: I love this scripture because God gives you wisdom, knowledge and happiness outside of him you will find none of that.

Assignment: Find your ONE good thing for today and write it down. (2 Corinthians 10:5)

_____

_____

Day 219

Isaiah 45:3

I will give you hidden treasures, riches stored
in secret places, so that you may know that I
am the Lord, the God of Israel, who summons
you by name.

Note from Carla: I love this scripture because God has
secret things that he wants to do just for you and no
one else just so that you can know he is Lord. One of
my personal best examples are requests that I have
asked God for that no one knew anything about and
then to see it happen exactly like my request as if me
God has this secret that one else was in on.

Assignment: Find your ONE good thing for today and write it
down. (2 Corinthians 10:5)

_____

_____

Day 220

Psalm 73:28

But as for me, it is good to be near God. I have made the Sovereign Lord my refuge; I will tell of all your deeds.

Note from Carla: When God delivers you and you know deep in your soul that if it had not been for God would you have perished you cannot keep quiet about God and all he has done. That is just a fact about this journey.

Assignment: Find your ONE good thing for today and write it down. (2 Corinthians 10:5)

_____

_____

Day 221

Proverbs 8:33-35

Listen to my instruction and be wise; do not disregard it. Blessed are those who listen to me, watching daily at my doors, waiting at my doorway. For those who find me find life and receive favor from the Lord.

Note from Carla: There are days when I feel like I am just sitting at his door waiting on him to open it and tell me what we are doing and then other days I feel like I am on a mission from God.

Assignment: Find your ONE good thing for today and write it down. (2 Corinthians 10:5)

_____

_____

Day 222

Psalm 86:6-7

Give ear, O Lord to my prayer, and Attend to the voice of my supplications. In the day of my trouble I will call upon you, for you will answer me.

Note from Carla: Talk it out with God, every day.

Assignment: Find your ONE good thing for today and write it down. (2 Corinthians 10:5)

_____

_____

Psalm 16:11

You make known to me the path of life; you
will fill me with joy in your presence, with
eternal pleasures at your right hand.

*Note from Carla: God has made it known the path of
life you just have to follow it and let his presence give
you joy.*

Assignment: Find your ONE good thing for today and write it
down. (2 Corinthians 10:5)

_____

_____

Ephesians 3:18-19

And I pray that you, being rooted and established in love, may have power, together with all the Lord's holy people, to grasp how wide and long and high and deep is the love of Christ, and to know this love that surpasses knowledge that you me be filled to the measure of all the fullness of God.

Assignment: Find your ONE good thing for today and write it down. (2 Corinthians 10:5)

_____

_____

Day 225

1 Chronicles 29:11

Yours, Lord is the greatness and the power and the glory and the majesty and the splendor, for everything in heaven and earth is yours. Yours, Lord is the kingdom; you are exalted as head over all.

Note from Carla; Song for your Playlist, Artist – Mercy Me, Song- I Can Only Imagine.

Assignment: Find your ONE good thing for today and write it down. (2 Corinthians 10:5)

_____

_____

Psalm 10:14

But you, God, see the trouble of the afflicted;
you consider their grief and take it in hand.
The victims commit themselves to you; you
are the helper of the fatherless.

Note from Carla: I LOVE this verse.

Assignment: Find your ONE good thing for today and write it
down. (2 Corinthians 10:5)

_____

_____

Day 227

Psalm 10:17

You Lord, hear the desire of the afflicted; you encourage them and you listen to their cry.

Note from Carla: just knowing that the Lord hears the desires of the afflicted and encourages them brings comfort even 227 days later.

Assignment: Find your ONE good thing for today and write it down. (2 Corinthians 10:5)

_____

_____

Day 228

John 15:5

I am the vine; you are the branches. If you remain in me and I in you, you will bear much fruit; apart from me you can do nothing.

Note from Carla; Song for your Playlist, Artist-Marvin Sapp, Song- Nothing Else Matters.

Assignment: Find your ONE good thing for today and write it down. (2 Corinthians 10:5)

_____

_____

Day 229

Revelation 2:10

Do not be afraid of what you are about to suffer. I tell you, the devil will put some of you in prison to test you, and you will suffer persecution for ten days. Be faithful, even to the point of death, and I will give you life as your victor's crown.

Note from Carla: No matter how dark the days you WILL come out victorious!

Assignment: Find your ONE good thing for today and write it down. (2 Corinthians 10:5)

_____

_____

Day 230

Psalm 73:23

Yet I am always with you; you hold me by my right hand. You guide me with your counsel and afterward you will take me into glory.

Note from Carla: I love this promise that He is always with me and he will guide me. There are so many things about this journey that I couldn't have predicted or expected but peace came from knowing he would guide me every step.

Assignment: Find your ONE good thing for today and write it down. (2 Corinthians 10:5)

_____

_____

Day 231

Ephesians 6:13

Therefore put on the full armor of God, so that when the day of evil comes, you may be able to stand your ground and after you have done everything to stand.

Note from Carla: What I love about this scripture is that God is so transparent, he flat out tells you when the day of evil comes! And then he tells you how to stand your ground! Simple instructions that is what I require.

Assignment: Find your ONE good thing for today and write it down. (2 Corinthians 10:5)

_____

_____

Day 232

1 Samuel 16:7

But the Lord said to Samuel, Don't judge by his appearance or height, for I have rejected him. The Lord doesn't see things the way you see them. People judge by outward appearance, but the Lord looks at the heart.

Note from Carla: This verse will hold you for LIFE! You can't look at what people do but you have to look at their intent and know that even if the world doesn't see it the Lord does! There is true peace in knowing that.

Assignment: Find your ONE good thing for today and write it down. (2 Corinthians 10:5)

_____

_____

Day 233

James 1:2

Consider it all joy, my brethren, when you encounter various trials, knowing that the testing of your faith produces endurance. And let endurance have its perfect result, so that you may be perfect and complete lacking in nothing.

Assignment: Find your ONE good thing for today and write it down. (2 Corinthians 10:5)

_____

_____

Day 234

Proverbs 16:3

Commit your works to the Lord and your plans will be established.

Note from Carla; Song for your Playlist today, Rev. Milton Brunson- Choir, Song-Way Maker.

Assignment: Find your ONE good thing for today and write it down. (2 Corinthians 10:5)

_____

_____

Psalm 34:15

The eyes of the Lord are on the righteous
and His ears are attentive to their cry.

*Note from Carla: Even on Day 235 the Lord is still
listening to you and he is watching over you.*

Assignment: Find your ONE good thing for today and write it
down. (2 Corinthians 10:5)

_____

_____

Day 236

Jeremiah 33:6

I will heal my people and will let them enjoy abundant peace and security.

Note from Carla: What a great promise from God! That he will heal me and give me peace and security.

Assignment: Find your ONE good thing for today and write it down. (2 Corinthians 10:5)

_____

_____

Day 237

Psalm 59:16

But I will sing of your strength, in the morning, I will sing of your love; for you are my fortress, my refuge in times of trouble.

Note from Carla: I don't sing except in the car but I will sing of his love and his strength!

Assignment: Find your ONE good thing for today and write it down. (2 Corinthians 10:5)

_____

_____

Day 238

Psalm 116:8-9

For you, Lord, have delivered me from death, my eyes from tears, my feet from stumbling, that I may walk before the Lord in the land of the living.

Note from Carla: I love that the Lord has delivered me daily from death and my eyes from tears daily so that I may walk in the land of the living.

Assignment: Find your ONE good thing for today and write it down. (2 Corinthians 10:5)

_____

_____

Day 239

Psalm 33:18

But the eyes of the Lord are on those who fear him. On those whose hope is in his unfailing love.

Note from Carla: Don't forget his eyes are on you!

Assignment: Find your ONE good thing for today and write it down. (2 Corinthians 10:5)

_____

_____

Day 240

Proverbs 16:9 (NLT)

We can make our plans, but the Lord determines our steps.

Note from Carla: Before I began this journey I felt pretty confident in my plans but now I know that the Lord truly determines my steps.

Assignment: Find your ONE good thing for today and write it down. (2 Corinthians 10:5)

_____

_____

Day 241

Matthew 6:20-21

But lay up for yourselves Treasures in heaven. For where your treasure is there will your heart be also.

Note from Carla: What I love about this verse is how deep it is even though it is simple. God tells you where to put your treasures so that they are eternal and not temporal. There are many things in this world that I have treasured but the one thing that is eternal is relationships.

Assignment: Find your ONE good thing for today and write it down. (2 Corinthians 10:5)

_____

_____

Day 242

Jeremiah 17:14

Heal Me Lord and I will be healed. Save me and I will be saved. For you are the one I praise.

Note from Carla; Song for your Playlist Today, Artist-Matthew West, Song-Broken Things.

Assignment: Find your ONE good thing for today and write it down. (2 Corinthians 10:5)

_____

_____

Day 243

Matthew 18:20

For where two or three gather in my name there am I with them.

Note from Carla: How I love the fact that God will be with me when I am alone but he will be there exponentially when I with other people.

Assignment: Find your ONE good thing for today and write it down. (2 Corinthians 10:5)

_____

_____

1 Timothy 4:8

For physical training is of some value, but Godliness has value for all things, holding promise for both the present life and the life to come.

Note from Carla; Song for your Playlist Today, Artist – Kari Jobe, Song – Forever.

Assignment: Find your ONE good thing for today and write it down. (2 Corinthians 10:5)

_____

_____

Day 245

Exodus 15:26

I am the Lord who heals You.

Note from Carla: Healing you mentally and spiritually are just as important as healing you physically.

Assignment: Find your ONE good thing for today and write it down. (2 Corinthians 10:5)

_____

_____

Day 246

Galatians 5:23

Gentleness and Self-Control against such things there is no law.

Note from Carla: Being gentle and using self-control when the world is so harsh and out of control can seem impossible.

Assignment: Find your ONE good thing for today and write it down. (2 Corinthians 10:5)

_____

_____

Day 247

Ephesians 4:32

Be Kind & Compassionate to one another,
forgiving each other, just as in Christ God
forgave you.

Note from Carla: We so often want compassion that
we are unwilling to give others. I think that is why
God had to remind us that he is the ultimate in
kindness and compassion and so no excuses!

Assignment: Find your ONE good thing for today and write it
down. (2 Corinthians 10:5)

_____

_____

Day 248

Joshua 1:7

Be Strong and courageous

Note from Carla: Just walking through a day can be you acting strong and courageous!

Assignment: Find your ONE good thing for today and write it down. (2 Corinthians 10:5)

_____

_____

Isaiah 43:1

Fear not: for I have redeemed you, I have called you by your name; you are mine.

Note from Carla: I love that God knows my name and that we are his!

Assignment: Find your ONE good thing for today and write it down. (2 Corinthians 10:5)

_____

_____

Day 250

1 Chronicles 28:20

Fear not, nor be dismayed for the Lord God will be with you; He will not fail you, nor forsake you!

Note from Carla: Even though it has been 250 days you still need daily reminders from God that you are not alone.

Assignment: Find your ONE good thing for today and write it down. (2 Corinthians 10:5)

_____

_____

Day 251

Psalm 46:2

Therefore we will not fear, though the earth be removed and though the mountains be carried into the sea.

Note from Carla; Song for your Playlist Today, Artist – Chris Tomlin, Song – Whom Shall I Fear.

Assignment: Find your ONE good thing for today and write it down. (2 Corinthians 10:5)

_____

_____

Day 252

Psalm 139: 13-14

You knit me in my mother's womb, I praise you because I am fearfully and wonderfully made; your works are wonderful, I know that full well.

Note from Carla: When I think about the detail that God went to in creating us all I stand in awe of his love and his work. We were complete in God's eyes before we were ever born!

Assignment: Find your ONE good thing for today and write it down. (2 Corinthians 10:5)

_____

_____

Day 253

1 Peter 1:6-7

In all this you greatly rejoice, though now for a little while you may have had to suffer grief in all kinds of trials. These have come so that the proven genuineness of your faith- of greater worth than gold, which perishes even though refined by fire may result in praise, glory and honor when Jesus Christ is revealed.

Assignment: Find your ONE good thing for today and write it down. (2 Corinthians 10:5)

_____

_____

Day 254

Ephesians 6:17

Take up....the sword of the spirit, which is the word of God and let's set the captives free!

Note from Carla: This journey can leave you in bondage, so strong that you may feel you will never be free but know that the sword of the spirit was given to you so that you could be free! USE IT!
Break off those chains!

Assignment: Find your ONE good thing for today and write it down. (2 Corinthians 10:5)

_____

_____

Day 255

Ephesians 5:15

Don't live foolishly as those with no understanding, but live honorably with true wisdom for we are living in evil times.

Note from Carla: Satan doesn't care how you feel he will kick you when you're down so be careful! Don't give him any extra chances to mess with you. Choose wisdom and walk with God.

Assignment: Find your ONE good thing for today and write it down. (2 Corinthians 10:5)

_____

_____

Proverbs 27:5

Better is open reprimand than concealed love.

Note from Carla: This verse kind of bothers me, only because being told your wrong just hurts. But it is truth that open correction is better than love that goes unsaid. You can't do better if you don't know better!

Assignment: Find your ONE good thing for today and write it down. (2 Corinthians 10:5)

_____

_____

Day 257

Proverbs 29:18

Where there is no vision, the people perish.

Note from Carla: You may feel like you have no vision since your new journey started. I can remember not planning anything out of reaction to what had happened. Then I got strong enough to plan a day ahead, then a week ahead, and then a month, I still struggle with a year out, I am hopeful the next year but I recognize it's all in God's hands.

Assignment: Find your ONE good thing for today and write it down. (2 Corinthians 10:5)

_____

_____

Day 258

Philippians 2:14-15

Do everything without complaining and arguing, so that no one can criticize you. Live clean, innocent lives as children of God, shining like bright lights in a world full of crooked and perverse people.

Note from Carla: I swear this verse just screams to our human nature! Because there is so much to complain about in this world but as a child of god you have to be a light in a dark place.

Assignment: Find your ONE good thing for today and write it down. (2 Corinthians 10:5)

_____

_____ .

Day 259

Psalm 91:4

He will cover you with this feathers. He will shelter you with his wings. His faithful promises are your armor and protection.

Note from Carla: I love the picture it paints of feathers. I guess because I love watching birds and how they are in their nests protecting their babies.

Assignment: Find your ONE good thing for today and write it down. (2 Corinthians 10:5)

_____

_____

Day 260

Psalm 27:2

When the wicked advance against me to devour me,
It is my enemies and my foes who swill stumble and fall.

Note from Carla: The wicked will advance against me but if I stand with God they will fall.

Assignment: Find your ONE good thing for today and write it down. (2 Corinthians 10:5)

_____

_____

Day 261

Psalm 27:3

Though an army besiege me, my heart will not fear; though war breakout against me, even then I will be confident.

Note from Carla: This journey brings many changes in your life and about now you may be starting to make changes that others just are not comfortable with. Maybe they have had you in a box and you are climbing out. Just know that if you stay hand in hand with God and walk where he says, you can be confident despite those who don't agree.

Assignment: Find your ONE good thing for today and write it down. (2 Corinthians 10:5)

_____

_____

Day 262

Psalm 27:5

For in the day of trouble he will keep me safe in his dwelling; he will hide me in the shelter of his sacred tent and set me high upon a rock.

Assignment: Find your ONE good thing for today and write it down. (2 Corinthians 10:5)

_____

_____

Day 263

Psalm 27:6

Then my head will be exalted above the enemies who surround me; at his sacred tent I will sacrifice with shouts of joy; I will sing and make music to the Lord.

Note from Carla: Song for your Playlist today. Whitney Houston – Song-Joy

Assignment: Find your ONE good thing for today and write it down. (2 Corinthians 10:5)

_____

_____

Day 264

Psalm 27:7

Hear my voice when I call, Lord; be merciful to me and answer me.

Note from Carla: You have no doubt called out to God many times over the past 264 days but no matter how many times he hears and he is merciful!

Assignment: Find your ONE good thing for today and write it down. (2 Corinthians 10:5)

_____

_____

Day 265

Psalm 27:13

I remain confident of this: I will see the goodness of the Lord in the land of the living.

Note from Carla: One of the blessings of this journey is that you become confident in one thing and is the goodness of God.

Assignment: Find your ONE good thing for today and write it down. (2 Corinthians 10:5)

_____

_____

Day 266

Psalm 27:14

Wait for the Lord; be strong and take heart and wait for the Lord.

Note from Carla: Waiting has been one of my greatest lessons, I am not a patient person but somehow I have learned to be patient for the Lord. In the waiting gives you strength that something bigger than you is happening.

Assignment: Find your ONE good thing for today and write it down. (2 Corinthians 10:5)

_____

_____

Day 267

Psalm 28:2

Hear my cry for mercy as I call to you for help, as I lift up my hands toward your most holy place.

Note from Carla; Song for your Playlist, Artist- Tamela Mann, Song – God Provides.

Assignment: Find your ONE good thing for today and write it down. (2 Corinthians 10:5)

_____

_____

Day 268

Psalm 29:11

The Lord gives strength to his people;
the Lord blesses his people with peace.

Note from Carla: Before this journey strength and peace meant something totally different to me. My strength was dependent on other people and how they treated me but now it is only dependent on the Lord and his peace.

Assignment: Find your ONE good thing for today and write it down. (2 Corinthians 10:5)

_____

_____

Day 269

Psalm 30:2-3

Lord my God, I called to you for help, and you healed me. You, Lord, brought me up from the realm of the dead; you spared me from going down to the pit.

Note from Carla: Song for your Playlist- Artist, Lauren Daigle, Song-"How can it be"

Assignment: Find your ONE good thing for today and write it down. (2 Corinthians 10:5)

_____

_____

Day 270

Psalm 31:1

In you, Lord, I have taken refuge; let me never be put to shame; deliver me in your righteousness.

Note from Carla: Taking refuge in the Lord is my only hope and I hope it is something that you have learned as well on this journey.

Assignment: Find your ONE good thing for today and write it down. (2 Corinthians 10:5)

_____

_____

Day 271

Psalm 31:9

Be merciful to me, Lord, for I am in distress; my eyes grow weak with sorrow, my soul and body with grief. My life is consumed by anguish and my years by groaning.

Note from Carla: Song for your Playlist today , Artists Brian & Jenn Johnson, Song – You're gonna be ok.

Assignment: Find your ONE good thing for today and write it down. (2 Corinthians 10:5)

_____

_____

Day 272

Psalm 31:19

How abundant are the good things that you have stored up for those who fear you, that you bestow in the sight of all, on those who take refuge in you.

Note from Carla: For all God has done he continues to give me sunshine, every day I see his love for me. Look for that one thing that God does for you every day that shows you he is still in love with you! For me it is the sunrise, and birds singing.

Assignment: Find your ONE good thing for today and write it down. (2 Corinthians 10:5)

_____

_____

Day 273

Psalm 32:8

I will instruct you and teach you in the way you should go; I will counsel you with my loving eye on you.

Note from Carla: One of the things that prevailed me on the journey was not knowing what to do and what way to go. But I found quickly that if I asked God he would tell me. We have a closed door policy. What I mean by that is I told God, You know me and you know I will walk through every open door so please shut the doors that I am not supposed to go through so I will know the right way! And man has he ever honored that request. Doors have slammed shut so loud that people who don't even know about my deal with good notice!

Assignment: Find your ONE good thing for today and write it down. (2 Corinthians 10:5)

_____

_____

Day 274

Psalm 33:20-22

We wait in hope for the Lord; he is our
help and our shield. In him our hearts
rejoice, for we trust in his holy name.
May your unfailing love be with us,
Lord, even as we put our hope in you.

Assignment: Find your ONE good thing for today and
write it down. (2 Corinthians 10:5)

_____

_____

Psalm 34:4

I sought the Lord, and he answered me; he delivered me from all of my fears.

Note from Carla: What peace God gives us when we give him all of our fears.

Assignment: Find your ONE good thing for today and write it down. (2 Corinthians 10:5)

_____

_____

Day 276

Psalm 34:18

The Lord is close to the brokenhearted and saves those who are crushed in spirit.

Note from Carla: Song for your Playlist, Artist – Tamela Mann, Song- Take me to the King.

Assignment: Find your ONE good thing for today and write it down. (2 Corinthians 10:5)

_____

_____

Day 277

Jeremiah 33:3

Call to me and I will answer you and tell you great and unsearchable things you do not know.

Note from Carla: What a promise, that he would tell us great and unsearchable things.

Assignment: Find your ONE good thing for today and write it down. (2 Corinthians 10:5)

_____

_____

Day 278

Ephesians 3:20

God will do exceedingly, abundantly above all that I ask or think. Because I honor him. His blessings will chase me down and overtake me. I will be in the right place at the right time. People will go out of their way to be good to me.

Note from Carla: What I LOVE is His Blessings will chase me down and overtake me!

Assignment: Find your ONE good thing for today and write it down. (2 Corinthians 10:5)

_____

_____

Day 279

Ecclesiastes 3:11

He has made everything beautiful in its time.
He has also set eternity in the human heart;
yet no one can fathom what God has done
from beginning to end.

*Note from Carla: Song for your playlist, Artist –
Mercy Me, Song – I can only imagine.*

Assignment: Find your ONE good thing for today and write it
down. (2 Corinthians 10:5)

_____

_____

Day 280

Ecclesiastes 7:13-14

Consider what God has done: Who can straighten what has been made crooked? When times are good, be happy; but when times are bad, consider this: God has made the one as well as the other. Therefore, no one can discover anything about their future.

Note from Carla: Today may you consider what God has done over the past 280, he has made the crooked way straight.

Assignment: Find your ONE good thing for today and write it down. (2 Corinthians 10:5)

_____

_____

Day 281

Deuteronomy 16:11

And rejoice before the Lord your God at the place he will choose as a dwelling for his Name- you, your sons, and daughters, your male and female servants, the Levites in your towns, and the foreigners, the fatherless and the widows living among you.

Note from Carla: What I love about this scripture is he calls me out by name! Widows.

Assignment: Find your ONE good thing for today and write it down. (2 Corinthians 10:5)

_____

_____

Day 282

Psalm 51:6

Yet you desired faithfulness even in the womb; you taught me wisdom in that secret place.

Note from Carla: Proof that Life began in the womb not on the day I was born! I love that God had relationship with me before I was born and will have one with me after my death.

Assignment: Find your ONE good thing for today and write it down. (2 Corinthians 10:5)

_____

_____

Psalm 122:7

Peace be within your walls and security within your towers! (MEV)

Note from Carla: If you are struggling with peace in your house pray this scripture.

Assignment: Find your ONE good thing for today and write it down. (2 Corinthians 10:5)

_____

_____

Proverbs 3:3

Let love and faithfulness never leave
you; bind them around your neck,
write them on the tablet of your heart.

*Note from Carla: No matter how dark the days
never let love and faithfulness leave you.*

Assignment: Find your ONE good thing for today and
write it down. (2 Corinthians 10:5)

_____

_____

Day 285

Psalm 38:21

Lord, do not forsake me; Do not be far from me, my God.

Note from Carla: This was my cry many days of this journey and if it has been your cry as well know that what you were asking for is biblical and while you may not feel God close he is and it is ok for you to cry out to him.

Assignment: Find your ONE good thing for today and write it down. (2 Corinthians 10:5)

_____

_____

Day 286

Lamentations 3:55-57

I called on your name, Lord, from the depths of the pit. You heard my plea: "Do not close your ears to my cry for relief." You came near when I called you, and you said "Do not Fear".

Note from Carla: Another promise that God still hears your cry for relief.

Assignment: Find your ONE good thing for today and write it down. (2 Corinthians 10:5)

_____

_____

Day 287

Ecclesiastes 7:2

It is better to go to a house of mourning than to go to a house of feasting, for death is the destiny of everyone; the living should take this to heart.

Note from Carla: I shared this scripture because I think it's important on this journey to embrace the fact that mourning is a part of living and that death is the destiny of everyone and if you become the voice of that in your circle of influence that's good because everyone needs to walk in awareness.

Assignment: Find your ONE good thing for today and write it down. (2 Corinthians 10:5)

_____

_____

Day 288

Jeremiah 31: 3-4

I have loved you with an everlasting love; I have drawn you with unfailing kindness. I will build you up again, and you Virgin Israel, will be rebuilt. Again you will take up your timbrels and go out to dance with the joyful.

Note from Carla: What I love about this scripture is God's promise that God will build me up again!

Assignment: Find your ONE good thing for today and write it down. (2 Corinthians 10:5)

_____

_____

Day 289

Psalm 126:5

Those who sow with tears will reap with songs of joy.

Note from Carla: Song for your playlist, Artist Kristine DeMarco, song-It is well

Assignment: Find your ONE good thing for today and write it down. (2 Corinthians 10:5)

_____

_____

Day 290

Psalm 130:5

I wait for the Lord, my whole being waits, And in his word I put my hope.

Note from Carla: And even at day 290 you may be waiting for your answer but put your hope in God.

Assignment: Find your ONE good thing for today and write it down. (2 Corinthians 10:5)

_____

_____

Psalm 131:3

Put your hope in the Lord both now and forevermore.

Note from Carla: You will forever put your hope in God after this journey.

Assignment: Find your ONE good thing for today and write it down. (2 Corinthians 10:5)

_____

_____

Day 292

Psalm 136:1

Give Thanks to the Lord for his is good.
His love endures forever.

Note from Carla: Song for your playlist today, Artist, Toby Mac – Song, Made to Love

Assignment: Find your ONE good thing for today and write it down. (2 Corinthians 10:5)

_____

_____

Day 293

Psalm 138:2

I will bow down toward your holy temple
and will praise your name for your unfailing
love and your faithfulness

Note from Carla: God's unfailing love and faithfulness will be your anthem on this journey.

Assignment: Find your ONE good thing for today and write it down. (2 Corinthians 10:5)

_____

_____

Day 294

Psalm 139:1

You have searched me, Lord, and you know me. You know when I sit and when I rise; you perceive my thoughts from afar.

Note from Carla: No one knows you like Jesus. You can fake it with all of your family and your friends but not with Jesus.

Assignment: Find your ONE good thing for today and write it down. (2 Corinthians 10:5)

_____

_____

Day 295

Psalm 143:5

I remember the days of long ago; I meditate on all your works and consider what your hands have done.

Note from Carla: Song for your Playlist today
: Artist, Donnie McClurkin, Song- I call you Faithful

Assignment: Find your ONE good thing for today and write it down. (2 Corinthians 10:5)

_____

_____

Day 296

Psalm 142:5

I cry to you Lord; I say, "You are my refuge, my portion in the land of living."

Note from Carla: This journey has taught me that I can cry out to God that he is my refuge and my portion.

Assignment: Find your ONE good thing for today and write it down. (2 Corinthians 10:5)

_____

_____

Day 297

Psalm 140:6

I say to the Lord, "You are my God"
Hear, Lord, my cry for mercy. Sovereign
Lord, my strong deliverer, you shield my
head in the day of battle.

Note from Carla: Whether Day 1 or Day 297 the Lord never grows weary of hearing your cry for mercy. He is your strong deliverer, your shield in the battle.

Assignment: Find your ONE good thing for today and write it down. (2 Corinthians 10:5)

_____

_____

Day 298

Psalm 143:10

Teach me to do your will, for you are my God; may your good Spirit lead me on level ground.

Note from Carla: God has to teach you to do his will it doesn't come naturally because you are made of flesh and bone.

Assignment: Find your ONE good thing for today and write it down. (2 Corinthians 10:5)

_____

_____

Day 299

Psalm 144:2

He is my loving God and my fortress, my
stronghold and my deliverer, my shield, in
whom I take refuge, who subdues peoples
under me.

Note from Carla: Song for your playlist today,
Artist Crowder, Song "All my Hope"

Assignment: Find your ONE good thing for today and write it
down. (2 Corinthians 10:5)

_____

_____

Day 300

Psalm 145:13-14

The Lord is trustworthy in all he promises and faithful in all he does. The Lord upholds all who fall and lifts up all who are bowed down.

Note from Carla: I pray you see the Lord is trustworthy and that he has upheld you and lifted you up.

Assignment: Find your ONE good thing for today and write it down. (2 Corinthians 10:5)

_____

_____

Day 301

Psalm 145:17-20

The Lord is righteous in all his ways and faithful in all he does. The Lord is near to all who call on him to all who call on him in truth. He fulfills the desires of those who fear him; he ears their cry and saves them. The Lord watches over all who love him, but all the wicked he will destroy.

Assignment: Find your ONE good thing for today and write it down. (2 Corinthians 10:5)

_____

_____

Day 302

Psalm 146:1-5

Praise the Lord. Praise the Lord, my soul. I will praise the Lord all my life; I will sing praise to my God as long as I live. Do not put your trust in princes, in human beings, who cannot save. When their spirit departs, they return to the ground; on that very day their plans come to nothing. Blessed are those whose help is the God of Jacob, whose hope is in the Lord their God.

Assignment: Find your ONE good thing for today and write it down. (2 Corinthians 10:5)

_____

_____

Day 303

Psalm 146:9

The Lord watches over the foreigner and sustains the fatherless and the widow, but he frustrates the ways of the wicked.

Note from Carla: Hard to believe that 303 days have passed since you started on this journey but it has and you have found new mercies

Assignment: Find your ONE good thing for today and write it down. (2 Corinthians 10:5)

_____

_____

Day 304

Psalm 147:5-6

Great is our Lord and might in power; his understanding has no limit. The Lord sustains the humble but casts the wicked to the ground.

Note from Carla: What I love about this scripture is his understanding has no limit!

Assignment: Find your ONE good thing for today and write it down. (2 Corinthians 10:5)

_____

_____

Day 305

Ephesians 6:18

And pray in the Spirit on all occasions with all kinds of prayers and requests. With this in mind, be alert and always keep on praying.

Note from Carla: Just keep praying! Keep talking to God!

Assignment: Find your ONE good thing for today and write it down. (2 Corinthians 10:5)

_____

_____

Day 306

Romans 12:15

Rejoice with those who rejoice; mourn with those who mourn.

Note from Carla: There is healing in crying with those who cry, so share in joy and pain.

Assignment: Find your ONE good thing for today and write it down. (2 Corinthians 10:5)

_____

_____

Day 307

1 John 5:14

This is the confidence we have in approaching God: that if we ask anything according to his will, he hears us.

Note from Carla: You can have confidence in approaching God that he will do what he says in his word.

Assignment: Find your ONE good thing for today and write it down. (2 Corinthians 10:5)

_____

_____

Day 308

Jeremiah 31:25

I will refresh the weary and satisfy the faint.

Note from Carla: God will refresh you! Let him!

Assignment: Find your ONE good thing for today and write it down. (2 Corinthians 10:5)

_____

_____

Day 309

Exodus 33:14

My presence will go with you, and I will give you rest.

Note from Carla: God promises to give you rest! So don't be afraid to rest in his presence.

Assignment: Find your ONE good thing for today and write it down. (2 Corinthians 10:5)

_____

_____

Day 310

2 Corinthians 4:6

For God, who said, "Let light shine out of darkness," has shown in our hearts to give the light of the knowledge of the glory of God.

Note from Carla: God has shown you his light in your darkness.

Assignment: Find your ONE good thing for today and write it down. (2 Corinthians 10:5)

_____

_____

Day 311

Romans 12:2

Do not conform to the pattern of this world, but be transformed by the renewing of your mind. Then you will be to test and approve what God's will is – his good, pleasing and perfect will.

Note from Carla: Be transformed today by the word of God!

Assignment: Find your ONE good thing for today and write it down. (2 Corinthians 10:5)

_____

_____

Day 312

Psalm 121:7

The Lord will keep you from all harm–

He will watch over your life.

Note from Carla: Although you have seen harm and you don't understand how this verse could be true God promises He will watch over your life.

Assignment: Find your ONE good thing for today and write it down. (2 Corinthians 10:5)

_____

_____

Day 313

Psalm 121:5

The Lord watches over you- the Lord is your shade at your right hand; the sun will not harm you by day, or the moon by night.

Note from Carla: For the next few days it may feel like the scriptures have a theme but these were the order in which God gave them to me so I pray that you understand he is watching over you.

Assignment: Find your ONE good thing for today and write it down. (2 Corinthians 10:5)

_____

_____

Day 314

Psalm 121:8

The Lord will watch over your coming and going both now and forevermore.

Note from Carla: You may feel very alone in your coming and going but the Lord is with you now and forever! So trust his word not your feelings.

Assignment: Find your ONE good thing for today and write it down. (2 Corinthians 10:5)

_____

_____

Day 315

Psalm 124:8

Our help is in the name of the Lord, the Maker of heaven and earth.

Note from Carla: Song for your playlist today: Third Day – Song "God of Wonders"

Assignment: Find your ONE good thing for today and write it down. (2 Corinthians 10:5)

_____

_____

Day 316

Psalm 125:1

Those who trust In the Lord are like Mount Zion, which cannot be shaken but endures forever.

Note from Carla: This journey has proven this verse to be true in my life, no one can shake my trust in the Lord,

Assignment: Find your ONE good thing for today and write it down. (2 Corinthians 10:5)

_____

_____

Day 317

Psalm 126:6

Those who go out weeping carrying seed to sow, will return with songs of joy, carrying sheaves with them.

Note from Carla: You may start out this journey weeping but you will return with songs of joy.

Assignment: Find your ONE good thing for today and write it down. (2 Corinthians 10:5)

_____

_____

Day 318

Psalm 130:1

Out of the depths I cry to you, Lord;
Lord, hear my voice. Let your ears be
attentive to my cry for mercy.

Note from Carla: Over the past 318 days I have shared scripture that say this very thing, none of them have been duplicates but all confirm that many have cried out to the Lord and you can too!

Assignment: Find your ONE good thing for today and write it down. (2 Corinthians 10:5)

_____

_____

Day 319

Psalm 100: 5

The Lord is good and his love endures forever; his faithfulness continues through all generations.

Note from Carla: Thank you Lord that he is good and his love endures forever.

Assignment: Find your ONE good thing for today and write it down. (2 Corinthians 10:5)

_____

_____

Day 320

2 Corinthians 5:17 (NIV)

Therefore, if anyone is in Christ, he is a new creation. The old has passed away; behold the new has come.

Note from Carla: Behold today the new has come, you are new today.

Assignment: Find your ONE good thing for today and write it down. (2 Corinthians 10:5)

_____

_____

Day 321

Psalm 8:1

Lord, our Lord, how majestic is your
name in all the earth! You have set your
glory in the heavens.

*Note from Carla: My hope for you this day is that you
will focus on how majestic the Lord is.*

Assignment: Find your ONE good thing for today and write it
down. (2 Corinthians 10:5)

_____

_____

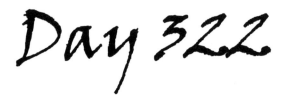

Day 322

Proverbs 3:6

In all your ways acknowledge Him, and He shall direct your paths."

Note from Carla: It is very simple acknowledge him and he WILL direct you on this journey every day.

Assignment: Find your ONE good thing for today and write it down. (2 Corinthians 10:5)

_____

_____

Day 323

Romans 12:6-8

We have different gifts, according to the grace given to each of us. If your gift is prophesying then prophesy in accordance with your faith; if it is serving, then serve; if it is teaching, then teach; if it is to encourage, then give encouragement; if it is giving, then give generously; if it is to lead, do it diligently; if it is to show mercy do it cheerfully.

Note from Carla: You remain here for a purpose! Do NOT lose sight of it!

Assignment: Find your ONE good thing for today and write it down. (2 Corinthians 10:5)

_____

_____

Day 324

Psalm 103:2

Let all that I am praise the Lord, with my whole heart, may I never forget the good things he does for me.

Note from Carla: Today you have 324 good things that he has done for you Praise him for them all!

Assignment: Find your ONE good thing for today and write it down. (2 Corinthians 10:5)

_____

_____

Day 325

Psalm 103:4-5

He redeems me from death and crowns me with love and tender mercies. He fills my life with good things. My youth is renewed like the eagles!

Note from Carla: Despite all of my loss he continues to fill my life with good things.

Assignment: Find your ONE good thing for today and write it down. (2 Corinthians 10:5)

_____

_____

Day 326

Psalm 7:17

I will give thanks to the Lord because of his righteousness; I will sing the praises of the name of the Lord Most High.

Note from Carla: Just give Thanks today.

Assignment: Find your ONE good thing for today and write it down. (2 Corinthians 10:5)

_____

_____

Day 327

Galatians 6:2

Carry each other's burdens and in this way you will fulfill the law of Christ.

Note from Carla: Through this journey you will carry each other's burdens differently than you ever have before. You will pray for and cry for others differently.

Assignment: Find your ONE good thing for today and write it down. (2 Corinthians 10:5)

_____

_____

Day 328

Philippians 1:6

Being confident of this very thing, that he which had begun a good work in you will perform it until the day of Jesus Christ.

Note from Carla... it ain't over till God says, so keep walking this journey to the end.

Assignment: Find your ONE good thing for today and write it down. (2 Corinthians 10:5)

_____

_____

Day 329

2 Peter 3:9

The Lord is not slow in keeping his promise, as some understand slowness. Instead he is patient with you, not wanting anyone to perish, but everyone to come to repentance.

Note from Carla: What I love about this scripture is that God is patient with me.

Assignment: Find your ONE good thing for today and write it down. (2 Corinthians 10:5)

_____

_____

Day 330

1 Peter 3:15

But in your hearts revere Christ as Lord. Always be prepared to give an answer to everyone who asks you to give the reason for the hope that you have.

Note from Carla: One thing that you will take away from this journey is your willingness to share where your hope comes from.

Assignment: Find your ONE good thing for today and write it down. (2 Corinthians 10:5)

_____

_____

2 Chronicles 16:9

For the eyes of the Lord move to and fro throughout the earth that he may strongly support those whose heart is completely His.

Note from Carla: God is constantly looking for ways he can support you!

Assignment: Find your ONE good thing for today and write it down. (2 Corinthians 10:5)

_____

_____

Day 332

2 Corinthians 4:18

So we fix our eyes not on what is seen, but on what is unseen, since what is seen is temporary, but what is unseen is eternal.

Note from Carla: If this journey teaches anything it is that what is seen is temporary but what is unseen is eternal.

Assignment: Find your ONE good thing for today and write it down. (2 Corinthians 10:5)

_____

_____

Day 333

2 Corinthians 5:7

For we live by faith, not by sight.

Note from Carla: If ever a journey taught me anything it was this verse that I will by faith and not by sight.

Assignment: Find your ONE good thing for today and write it down. (2 Corinthians 10:5)

_____

_____

Day 334

Isaiah 49:8

This is what the Lord Says: "In the time of my favor I will answer you, and in the day of salvation I will help you; I will keep you and will make you to be a covenant for the people, to restore the land and to reassign its desolate inheritances.

Note from Carla: What I love about this scripture is God's promise to restore the land and to reassign its desolate inheritances. Don't kid yourself God is keeping score and he will take care of his children.

Assignment: Find your ONE good thing for today and write it down. (2 Corinthians 10:5)

_____

_____

Day 335

Hosea 14:7

They that dwell under his shadow shall return; they shall revive as the grain, and blossom as the vine: the scent thereof shall be as the wine of Lebanon.

Note from Carla: Although this scripture may be referring to things that seem unfamiliar the truth is in the verbs, if you dwell with him you will be revived.

Assignment: Find your ONE good thing for today and write it down. (2 Corinthians 10:5)

_____

_____

Day 336

Psalm 91:1

He that dwelleth in the secret place of the Most High Shall abide under the shadow of the Almighty.

Note from Carla: If during your sorrow you have found yourself dwelling in the secret place of the most high you know this incredible scripture.

Assignment: Find your ONE good thing for today and write it down. (2 Corinthians 10:5)

_____

_____

Day 337

Psalm 138:7

Though I walk in the midst of trouble, thou wilt revive me; Thou wilt stretch forth they hand against the wrath of mine enemies, And thy right hand will save me.

Assignment: Find your ONE good thing for today and write it down. (2 Corinthians 10:5)

_____

_____

Day 338

Psalm 90:12

So teach us to number our days, that we may get us a heart of wisdom.

Note from Carla: One of the many blessings of this journey is the knowledge that you now know Life is finite and there is a specific number to the days you are given, with that comes wisdom to make the most of each day because while you know life is finite you don't know what your number is.

Assignment: Find your ONE good thing for today and write it down. (2 Corinthians 10:5)

_____

_____

Day 339

Matthew 5:12

Rejoice, and be exceeding glad: for great is your reward in heaven; for so persecuted they the prophets that were before you.

Note from Carla: Two things I love about this verse, First is that the Lord says to be glad because he has your reward waiting for you and second is that he reminds you if you are persecuted you are not and were not alone in it.

Assignment: Find your ONE good thing for today and write it down. (2 Corinthians 10:5)

_____

_____

Day 340

Romans 5:3

And not only so, but we also rejoice in our tribulations; knowing that tribulation worketh steadfastness;

Note from Carla: If ever you have proven this scripture true this journey has that through your tribulation God is working out your steadfast hope in him!

Assignment: Find your ONE good thing for today and write it down. (2 Corinthians 10:5)

_____

_____

Day 341

Exodus 6:6

I am God. I will bring you out from under
the cruel hard labor of Egypt. I will rescue
you from slavery. I will redeem you,
intervening with great acts of judgment.

*Note from Carla: I love this verse because God is
specific in his promise to bring you out, rescue you, and
redeem you.*

Assignment: Find your ONE good thing for today and write it
down. (2 Corinthians 10:5)

_____

_____

Day 342

Psalm 78:35

And they remembered that God was their rock, and the most high God their redeemer.

Note from Carla: After 342 days on this journey you will never forget that God is your rock and the most high. One of the things that this journey does for you is give you a resolve about who God is and what he can do!

Assignment: Find your ONE good thing for today and write it down. (2 Corinthians 10:5)

_____

_____

Day 343

Psalm 124:1-5

If God had not been for us – all together now, Israel, sing out! – If God hadn't been for us when everyone went against us, we would have been swallowed alive by their violent anger, Swept away by the flood of rage, drowned in the torrent; we would have lost our lives in the wild, raging water.

Assignment: Find your ONE good thing for today and write it down. (2 Corinthians 10:5)

_____

_____

Day 344

Philippians 3:12

Not that I have already obtained, or am already made perfect: but I press on, if so be that I may lay hold on that for which also I was laid hold on by Christ Jesus.

Note from Carla: One thing that I have become very aware of through this journey is how flawed I am, and that despite my flaws God will use me if I just press on.

Assignment: Find your ONE good thing for today and write it down. (2 Corinthians 10:5)

_____

_____

Day 345

Philippians 4:8-9

Whatsoever things are true, whatsoever things are honorable, whatsoever things are just, whatsoever things are purse, whatsoever things are lovely, whatsoever things are of good report, if there be any virtue, and if there be any praise, think on these things. The things which ye both learned and received and heard and saw in me, these things do: and the God of peace shall be with you.

Assignment: Find your ONE good thing for today and write it down. (2 Corinthians 10:5)

_____

_____

Day 346

1 Peter 4:8

Above all, love each other deeply, because love covers over a multitude of sins.

Note from Carla: During this journey there are many things that are said out of hurt and pain so it's important to remember to love those you have deeply and know it covers a multitude of sins.

Assignment: Find your ONE good thing for today and write it down. (2 Corinthians 10:5)

_____

_____

Day 347

Psalm 40:1-2

I waited patiently for the Lord; he turned to me and heard my cry. 2. He lifted me out of the slimy pit, out of the mud and mire; he set my feet on a rock and gave me a firm place to stand.

Assignment: Find your ONE good thing for today and write it down. (2 Corinthians 10:5)

_____

_____

Day 348

Psalm 41:1-2

Blessed are those who have regard for the weak; the LORD delivers them in times of trouble.

2 The LORD protects and preserves them— they are counted among the blessed in the land— he does not give them over to the desire of their foes.

Assignment: Find your ONE good thing for today and write it down. (2 Corinthians 10:5)

_____

_____

Day 349

Lamentations 3:32

Though he brings grief, he will show compassion, so great is his unfailing love. For he does not willingly bring affliction or grief to anyone.

Note from Carla: A song for your playlist, Hillary Scott, "Thy Will"

Assignment: Find your ONE good thing for today and write it down. (2 Corinthians 10:5)

_____

_____

Day 350

2 Corinthians 1:3-4

Praise be to the God and Father of our Lord Jesus Christ, the Father of compassion and the God of all comfort, 4 who comforts us in all our troubles, so that we can comfort those in any trouble with the comfort we ourselves receive from God.

Assignment: Find your ONE good thing for today and write it down. (2 Corinthians 10:5)

_____

_____

Day 351

Proverbs 12:25

Anxiety weighs down the heart, but a kind word cheers it up.

Note from Carla: Amazing how a kind word changes everything! Don't forget your kind words matter as well.

Assignment: Find your ONE good thing for today and write it down. (2 Corinthians 10:5)

_____

_____

Psalm 43:2

You are God my stronghold.

Note from Carla: For this year journey
knowing where your stronghold is changes
everything.

Assignment: Find your ONE good thing for today and write it
down. (2 Corinthians 10:5)

_____

_____

Day 353

Hosea 6:1

Come, let us return to the Lord. He has torn us to pieces but he will heal us; he has injured us but he will bind up our wounds.

Note from Carla: When it says he has torn us to pieces I believe this means that the order of things that the Lord created such as death has torn us to pieces but God will heal us. He knew when death came into the world that we would be injured and torn up over it and so he promised to heal us and bind up our wounds.

Assignment: Find your ONE good thing for today and write it down. (2 Corinthians 10:5)

_____

_____

Day 354

Psalm 5:11

But let all who take refuge in you be glad; let them ever sing for joy. Spread your protection over them, that those who love your name may rejoice in you.

Note from Carla: May you find joy in the journey.

Assignment: Find your ONE good thing for today and write it down. (2 Corinthians 10:5)

_____

_____

Day 355

Romans 12:11

Never be lacking in zeal, but keep your spiritual fervor, serving the Lord.

Note from Carla: The spirit inside of you is stronger than your flesh so keep your focus on your spirit side serving the Lord and you will not be lacking in excitement.

Assignment: Find your ONE good thing for today and write it **down.** (2 Corinthians 10:5)

_____

_____

Day 356

Psalm 47:1-2

Clap your hands, all you nations; shout to God with cries of joy. For the Lord Most High is awesome, the great King over all the earth.

Note from Carla: I have heard people say, "Oh I can't do that I am quiet and reserved." Seriously!! You may be to the rest of the world but God knows you! And when you are in the presence of the creator of the universe you will clap your hands and shout!

Assignment: Find your ONE good thing for today and write it down. (2 Corinthians 10:5)

_____

_____

Day 357

Psalm 19:14
May these words of my mouth and this
meditation of my heart be pleasing in your
sight, lord, my rock and my redeemer.

*Note from Carla: Another song for your Playlist,
Artist Nicole C. Mullen, song —My Redeemer Lives*

Assignment: Find your ONE good thing for today and write it
down. (2 Corinthians 10:5)

_____

_____

Day 358

Jeremiah 1:5

Before you saw the Light of Day, I had holy plans for you...

Note from Carla: Before you started on this journey God had Holy plans for you.

Assignment: Find your ONE good thing for today and write it down. (2 Corinthians 10:5)

_____

_____

Day 359

Psalm 16:5

Lord, you alone are my portion and my cup; you make my lot secure.

Note from Carla: Today will start your week before... What I mean is today starts the week before your loss a year ago and what I experienced is re-living the moments before my life changed forever. So know if you do that as well it is very normal. But the Lord is your portion and will make you secure.

Assignment: Find your ONE good thing for today and write it down. (2 Corinthians 10:5)

_____

_____

Day 360

Psalm 38:15

For in Thee, O Lord, do I Hope;

Note from Carla: As you walk this last week of your year journey remember that your Good thing may come from the memories you have of this week a year ago.

Assignment: Find your ONE good thing for today and write it down. (2 Corinthians 10:5)

_____

_____

Day 361

Ephesians 1:7

He is so rich in kindness and grace that he purchased our freedom with the blood of his Son and forgave our sins.

Note from Carla: No matter what comes today remember that God purchased your freedom!

Assignment: Find your ONE good thing for today and write it down. (2 Corinthians 10:5)

_____

_____

Psalm 16:7

I will praise the Lord, who counsels me, even at night my heart instructs me.

Note from Carla: What a year of seeking God for counsel and this year has laid a foundation for you that is stronger in your faith and pursuit of God for counsel.

Assignment: Find your ONE good thing for today and write it down. (2 Corinthians 10:5)

_____

_____

Day 363

Psalm 119:45
I will walk about in freedom, for I have
sought out your precepts.

*Note from Carla: May today you walk in Freedom
that your loved one is seeing the things you have
hoped for and one day you will be with them again.*

Assignment: Find your ONE good thing for today and write it
down. (2 Corinthians 10:5)

_____

_____

Day 364

1 John 1:5

This is the message we have heard from Him and declare to you: God is light; in Him there is no darkness at all.

Note from Carla: God is your Light in the darkness.

Assignment: Find your ONE good thing for today and write it down. (2 Corinthians 10:5)

_____

_____

Day 365

Ephesians 6:10

Finally, be strong in the Lord and in his mighty power.

Note from Carla: Well we did it!! We made it through a whole year together! Blessings to you as you continue to walk out your new life. Cool thing is you now have a gratitude journal to keep and remind yourself of the year that was your first and how God made himself known to you during this year. Prayers, Hugs & Love to you and your new life!

Last song for the Playlist: Artist Marvin Sapp, Song-Never would have made it.

Assignment: Find your ONE good thing for today and write it down. (2 Corinthians 10:5)

_____

_____

Made in the USA
Lexington, KY
20 July 2018